VISUAL THINKING

Dr Gareth Moore B.Sc (Hons) M.Phil Ph.D is the internationally best-selling author of a wide range of brain-training and puzzle books for both children and adults, including *Enigma: Crack the Code*, *Ultimate Dot to Dot*, *Brain Games for Clever Kids*, *Lateral Logic* and *Extreme Mazes*. His books have sold millions of copies in the UK alone, and have been published in over thirty different languages. He is also the creator of online brain-training site BrainedUp.com, and runs the daily puzzle site PuzzleMix.com.

Find him online at DrGarethMoore.com

VISUAL THINKING

OPTICAL PUZZLES TO BOOST YOUR BRAIN POWER

DR GARETH MOORE

Michael O'Mara Books Limited

First published in Great Britain in 2021 by
Michael O'Mara Books Limited
9 Lion Yard
Tremadoc Road
London SW4 7NQ

A CIP catalogue record for this book is available from the British Library.

Papers used by Michael O'Mara Books Limited are natural, recyclable
products made from wood grown in sustainable forests. The manufacturing
processes conform to the environmental regulations of the country of origin.

ISBN: 978-1-78929-319-7 in paperback print format

1 2 3 4 5 6 7 8 9 10

Designed and typeset by Gareth Moore

Printed and bound by CPI Group (UK) Ltd, Croydon, CR0 4YY

www.mombooks.com

MIX
Paper from
responsible sources
FSC® C020471
FSC
www.fsc.org

INTRODUCTION

Welcome to *Visual Thinking*, packed full of over 30 different types of challenge, with a huge range of more than 300 puzzles to confuse and delight you in equal measure.

Ranging from non-verbal reasoning through to colouring puzzles that reveal a hidden picture when solved, there's something here for everyone. Whether you want to build your visualization skills, test your abilities or simply have some relaxing fun you'll find something suited to you. For the best mental benefit, however, you should be sure to try all of the different types of puzzle – even those that seem the trickiest, since these are likely to be the ones that will be most beneficial for your brain.

The puzzles are not arranged in any particular order, so feel free to dip in as you please. On average the harder puzzles are towards the back, although that's not always the case.

All of the puzzles are observation-based, but what you then do with those observations varies from challenge to challenge. In some cases you merely need to spot relevant details, whereas in others you will need to make logical deductions based on those observations. For all of the latter type of puzzle, full written explanations are provided in the solution section at the back of the book, so you should never be left wondering why an answer is deemed correct! Solutions are also given for all other puzzles, too.

Have fun!

Dr Gareth Moore

SHAPE COUNTING

How many squares and/or rectangles can you count in this image? Many of them will overlap, including the large rectangle all around the outside.

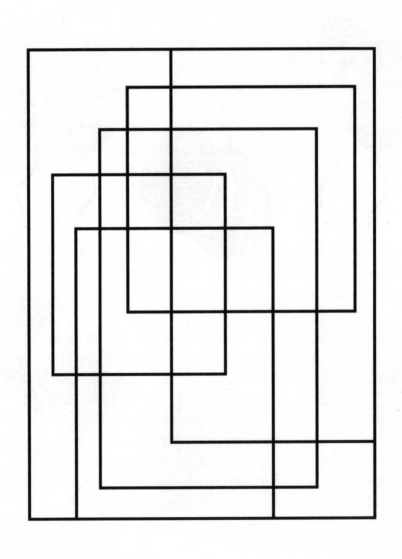

PAIRING PROBLEM

2

Join these balloons into identical pairs, allowing for rotation.

A

B

C

D

E

F

CUBIC CONUNDRUM

How many cubes are there in the following image? It began as a 5×4×4 block before some cubes were removed. None of the cubes are 'floating' in mid-air.

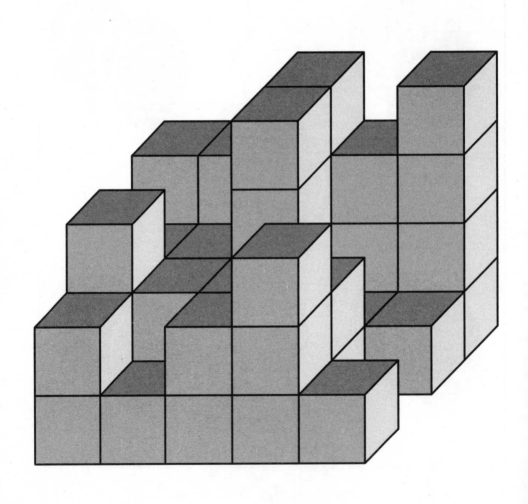

COLOUR BY PIXEL

Colour each square according to the key, to reveal a colourful hidden picture.

1	1	1	1	2	2	2	2	2	2	2	2	2	2	2	2	1	1	1	1
1	1	1	2	3	3	3	3	3	3	3	3	3	3	3	3	2	1	1	1
1	1	2	3	3	3	4	3	3	3	3	3	4	3	3	3	3	2	1	1
1	2	5	5	5	5	5	5	5	5	5	5	5	5	5	5	4	5	5	2	1
2	3	5	5	4	5	5	5	5	4	5	5	5	5	5	5	5	5	3	2
2	5	4	3	3	3	3	3	3	3	3	3	4	3	3	3	3	3	5	2
2	5	5	5	5	5	4	5	5	5	5	5	5	5	4	5	5	5	5	2
1	2	2	2	2	2	2	2	2	2	2	2	2	2	2	2	2	2	2	1
6	6	6	6	6	6	6	6	7	7	7	7	6	6	6	6	6	6	6	6
1	8	8	8	8	8	4	4	4	4	8	8	4	4	4	8	5	8	8	1
5	5	8	5	5	4	5	8	8	4	4	4	8	8	5	5	8	5	8	8
7	8	8	8	8	8	8	8	8	8	8	8	8	8	8	8	8	8	8	7
1	7	9	9	7	9	7	4	5	5	5	5	4	7	7	9	7	7	9	7
9	7	5	5	5	7	7	9	7	9	7	7	9	7	9	5	5	9	7	9
7	7	2	2	2	2	2	2	2	2	2	2	2	2	2	2	2	2	1	7
1	2	5	5	5	5	5	5	5	5	5	5	5	5	5	5	5	5	2	1
2	3	3	3	3	3	3	3	3	3	3	3	3	3	3	3	3	3	3	2
2	3	3	5	5	5	5	5	5	5	5	5	5	5	5	5	3	3	3	2
1	2	3	3	3	3	3	3	3	3	3	3	3	3	3	3	3	3	2	1
1	1	2	2	2	2	2	2	2	2	2	2	2	2	2	2	2	2	1	1

1 – light blue
2 – black
3 – orange
4 – yellow
5 – light orange
6 – red
7 – green
8 – brown
9 – light green

SHIP SHAPE

Which of the images, A to F, exactly matches a portion of the main image?

A

B

C

D
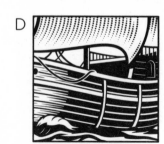

E

F

VISUAL THINKING

Imagine folding and then punching paper as shown. Unfold, and which image results?

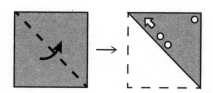

  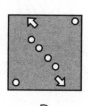 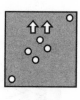

A   B   C   D   E

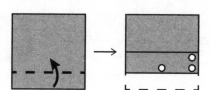

A   B   C   D   E

VISUAL THINKING

CRACK THE CODE

Crack the code used to describe each image, and circle the correct identifier for the image on the second line of each puzzle.

VB   PS   PB   VN   PN

    BN   VS   SP   VP   PP

URE   AMO   TMO   ARE   TME

  = ARM   TRO   UME   URO   URE

Which of the options, A to D, is an exact mirror image of the jet plane?

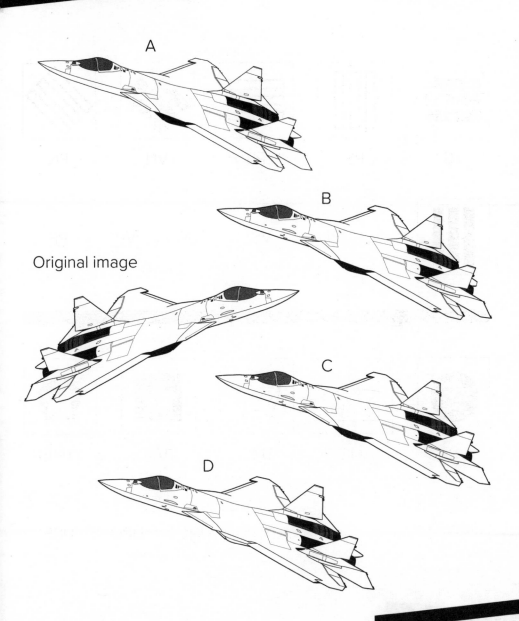

A

B

Original image

C

D

9

Join the dots with straight lines in increasing numerical order, starting at '1' (marked with a star), to reveal a hidden picture.

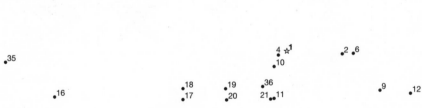

VISUAL THINKING

Which of the options, A to E, should be placed into the empty box in order to complete the pattern?

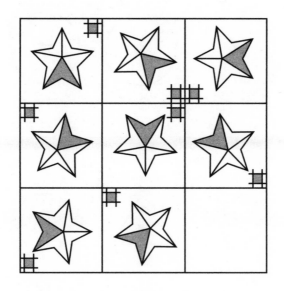

A

B

C

D

E

ODD ONE OUT

Which image is the odd one out on each line?

A   B   C   D   E

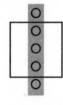

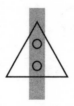
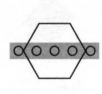

A   B   C   D   E

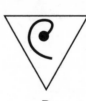

A   B   C   D   E

VISUAL THINKING

Which of the patterns, A to D, could
be cut out and folded to match the
view shown at the top?

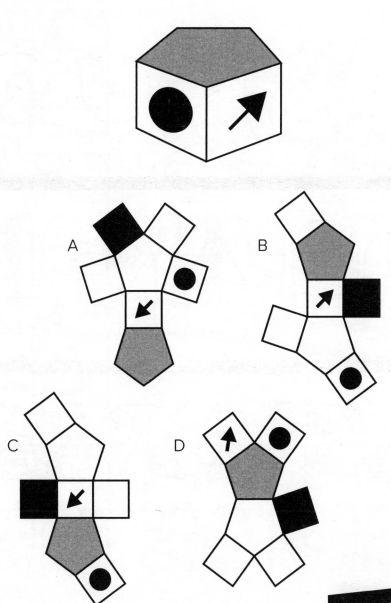

CAKE CUT

Which of the images, A to F, exactly matches a portion of the main image?

A

B

C

D

E

F

Imagine folding and then punching paper as shown. Unfold, and which image results?

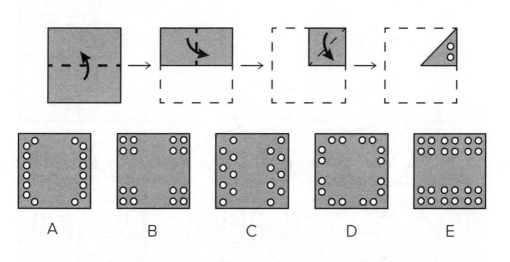

A   B   C   D   E

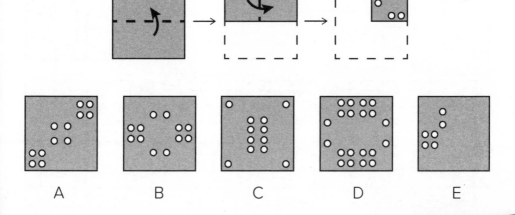

A   B   C   D   E

RECTANGLE MAZE

Find your way through the maze.

Which option, from A to E, should replace the question mark symbols in order to continue each sequence?

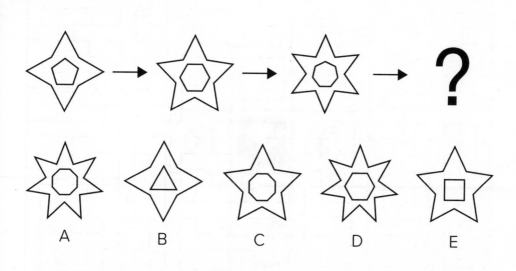

A   B   C   D   E

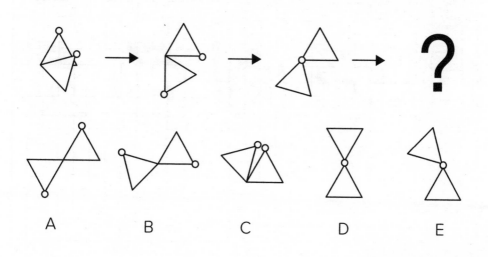

A   B   C   D   E

INCORRECT CUBE

If you were to cut out and fold this image to make a six-sided cube, which of the cube images beneath, A to E, could not be formed?

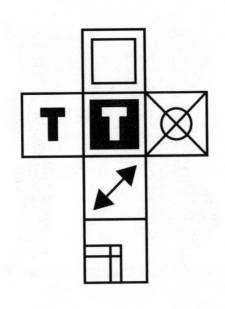

A   B   C   D   E

VISUAL THINKING

MATCHING HALVES

Join the eight halves together to make four complete cars.

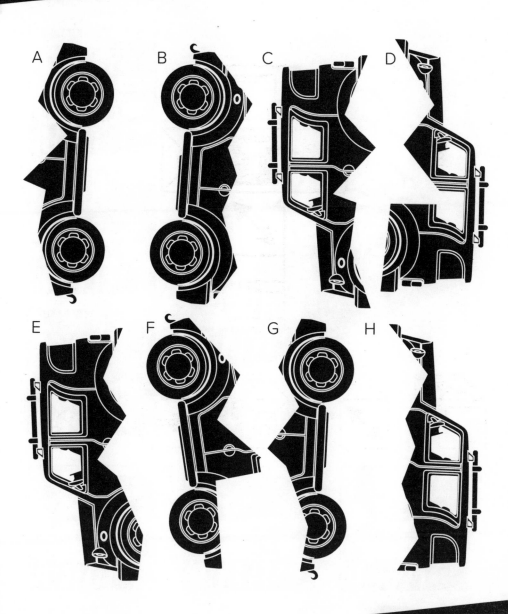

A B C D

E F G H

STEAMED OUT

Which of the images, A to F, exactly matches a portion of the main image?

A

B

C

D

E

F

FOLD AND PUNCH

Imagine folding and then punching paper as shown. Unfold, and which image results?

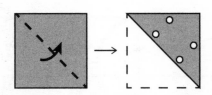

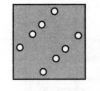

A   B   C   D   E

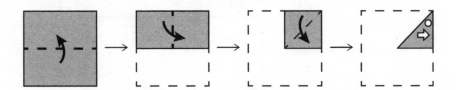

A   B   C   D   E

VISUAL THINKING

SHAPE COUNTING

How many squares and/or rectangles can you count in this image? Many of them will overlap, including the large rectangle all around the outside.

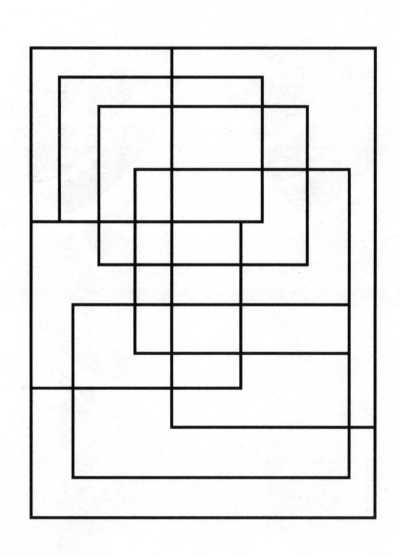

Join these cakes into identical pairs, allowing for rotation.

A

B

C

D

E

F

DOT TO DOT

Join the dots with straight lines in increasing numerical order, starting at '1' (marked with a star), to reveal a hidden picture.

Which of the options, A to E, should be placed into the empty box in order to complete the pattern?

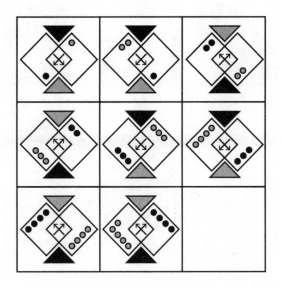

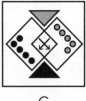

A   B   C   D   E

VISUAL THINKING

ODD ONE OUT

Which image is the odd one out on each line?

| A | B | C | D | E |

| A | B | C | D | E |

| A | B | C | D | E |

VISUAL THINKING

Which of the patterns, A to D, could be cut out and folded to match the view shown at the top?

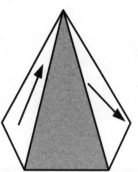

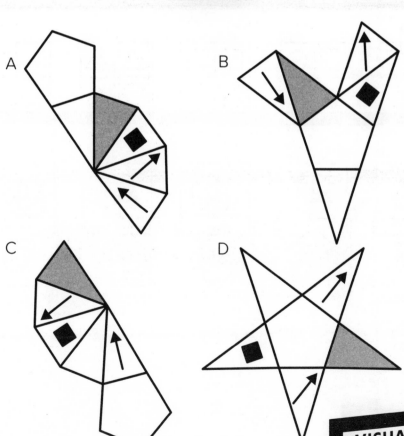

A

B

C

D

CRACK THE CODE

Crack the code used to describe each image, and circle the correct identifier for the image on the second line of each puzzle.

OGL · · · · · RGB · · · · · OEB · · · · · UEL · · · · · RFB

 = REL · · · OFL · · · RGL · · · UEB · · · UFL

ECX · · · · · NJH · · · · · SJX · · · · · NCX · · · · · OJH

 = NCX · · · OCH · · · EJH · · · SJH · · · ECH

Which of the options, A to E, is an exact mirror image of the giraffe?

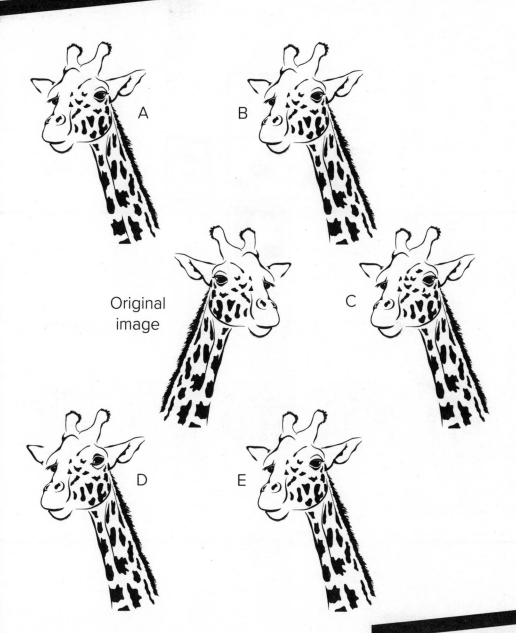

A

B

Original image

C

D

E

SPOT THE CUBE

If you were to cut out and fold this image to make a six-sided cube, which of the cube images beneath, A to E, is the only one that could be formed?

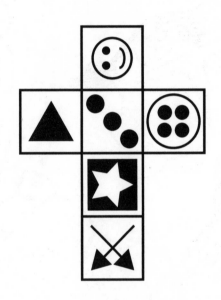

A B C D E

VISUAL
THINKING

Which two of these backpacks are identical, allowing for rotation?

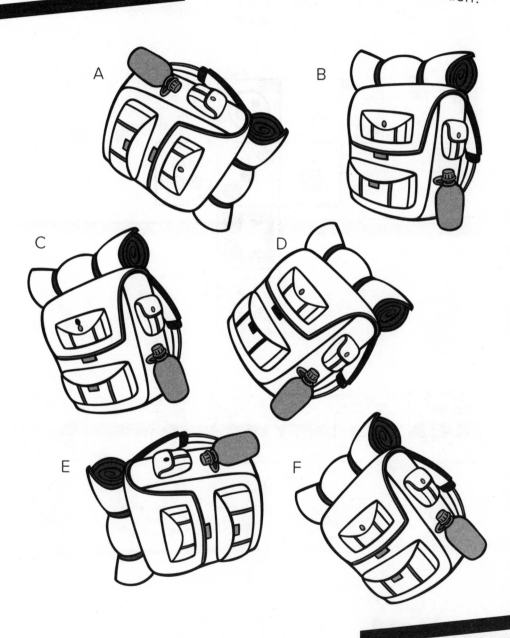

A

B

C

D

E

F

HIDDEN IMAGE

Which of the options, A to D, conceals the image shown on the far left of each row? It may be rotated but all elements of it must be visible.

A   B   C   D

 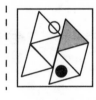

A   B   C   D

A   B   C   D

VISUAL THINKING

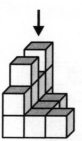

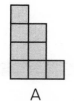 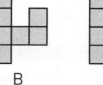   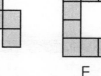

TOP VIEW

32

Which of the options, A to E, represents the view of the 3D object when seen from the direction of the arrow?

A   B   C   D   E

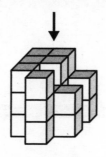

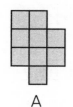

A   B   C   D   E

VISUAL THINKING

33 CUBIC CONUNDRUM

How many cubes are there in the following image? It began as a 5×4×4 block before some cubes were removed. None of the cubes are 'floating' in mid-air.

COLOUR BY PIXEL

Colour each square according to the key, to reveal a colourful hidden picture.

1	1	2	2	2	1	1	3	3	3	3	3	3	1	1	2	2	2	1	1
1	2	2	1	1	3	3	4	4	4	4	3	5	3	3	1	1	2	2	1
2	2	1	3	3	6	6	7	6	6	6	3	5	5	5	3	3	1	2	2
2	1	3	5	8	3	6	7	7	7	6	7	3	3	5	3	4	3	1	2
2	1	3	5	5	3	3	6	7	7	7	6	7	7	3	4	4	3	3	2
2	3	5	5	5	8	3	6	6	7	7	7	6	7	7	7	3	8	3	1
1	3	5	5	5	5	8	3	3	6	7	7	7	6	7	3	9	8	3	1
3	4	3	9	9	5	8	8	8	3	7	7	7	6	7	3	9	8	8	3
3	4	4	3	9	8	8	8	8	3	6	7	6	7	7	3	9	9	8	3
3	7	6	3	9	9	9	3	3	6	7	7	6	7	7	3	9	9	5	3
3	6	7	6	3	3	9	3	6	7	7	7	7	6	7	7	3	3	3	3
3	6	7	7	6	6	3	8	3	7	7	7	7	7	6	7	7	6	4	3
3	4	6	7	7	7	6	3	6	6	3	3	3	7	7	6	6	6	4	3
1	3	4	6	7	7	6	6	7	3	5	5	8	3	7	7	7	4	3	1
1	3	4	6	6	7	7	7	7	3	5	5	8	3	7	7	7	4	3	1
1	1	3	7	7	6	7	7	7	6	3	9	5	8	3	4	4	3	1	2
2	1	3	4	4	7	6	6	6	7	3	9	8	8	3	4	3	3	1	2
2	1	1	3	3	4	4	7	7	7	4	3	9	8	3	3	3	1	2	2
1	2	1	1	1	3	3	4	4	4	3	9	9	3	3	1	1	2	2	1
1	1	2	2	2	1	1	3	3	3	3	3	3	1	1	2	2	2	1	1

1 – light grey
2 – grey
3 – black
4 – dark blue

5 – dark green
6 – light blue
7 – blue
8 – green

9 – yellow

VISUAL THINKING

Which of the options, A to E, represents the view of the image shown at the top when folded in half along the dashed line? Assume it has been drawn on transparent paper.

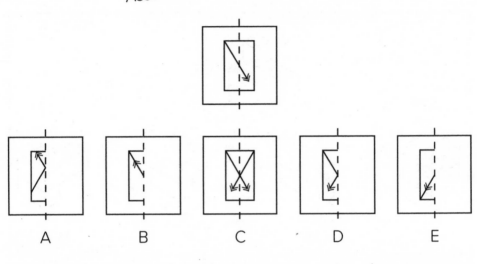

A   B   C   D   E

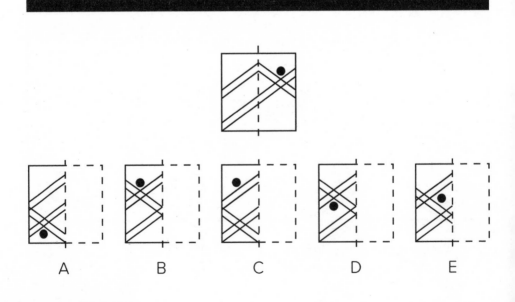

A   B   C   D   E

VISUAL THINKING

A NEW VIEW

Which of the options, A to D, represents a view of the first 3D object when seen from the direction of the arrow?

A

B

C

D

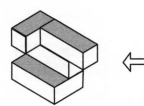

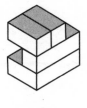

A

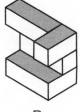

B

C

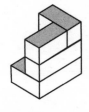

D

UPON REFLECTION

Which of the options, A to E, would result when each image is reflected in the dashed line shown?

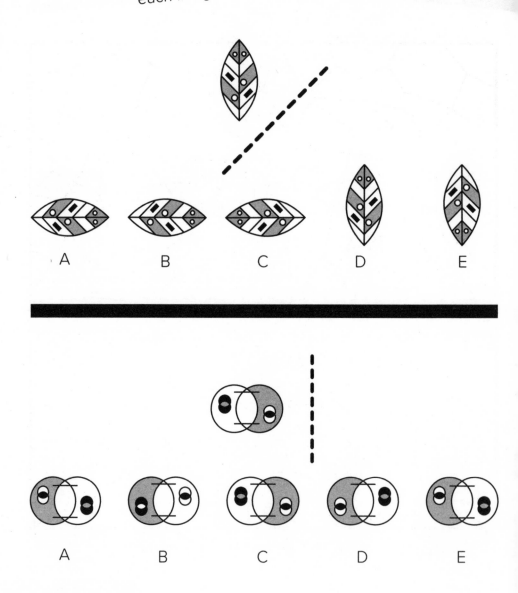

A   B   C   D   E

A   B   C   D   E

COLOUR BY SHAPE

Colour each shape according to the key, to reveal a colourful hidden picture.

1 – light green

2 – green

3 – dark green

4 – light grey

5 – grey

6 – dark grey

7 – light brown

8 – brown

9 – dark brown

0 – white

A – orange

B – red

VISUAL THINKING

39

BUILDING BLOCKS

Which of the sets of blocks, A to D, can be rearranged to form the assembly shown? All blocks must be used exactly once each.

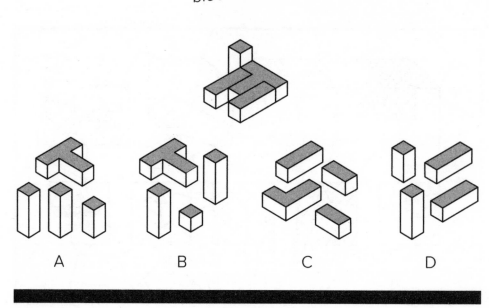

A   B   C   D

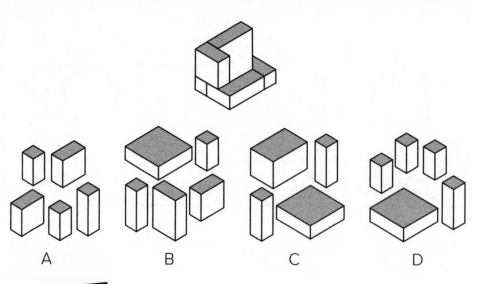

A   B   C   D

VISUAL THINKING

MISSING FACE

Which of the options, A to E, should replace the blank face on the cube so that they all become different views of the same cube? The correct face may need rotating.

A   B   C   D   E

A   B   C   D   E

VISUAL THINKING

41

ELEPHANT ENIGMA

Which of the images, A to F, exactly matches a portion of the main image?

A
B
C

D

E
F

Imagine folding and then punching paper as shown. Unfold, and which image results?

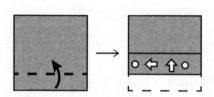

A   B   C   D   E

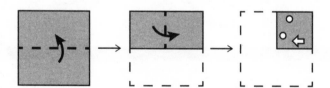

A   B   C   D   E

HIDDEN IMAGE

Which of the options, A to D, conceals the image shown on the far left of each row? It may be rotated but all elements of it must be visible.

A　　　B　　　C　　　D

A　　　B　　　C　　　D

   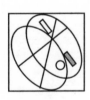

A　　　B　　　C　　　D

VISUAL
THINKING

Which of the options, A to E, represents the view of the 3D object when seen from the direction of the arrow?

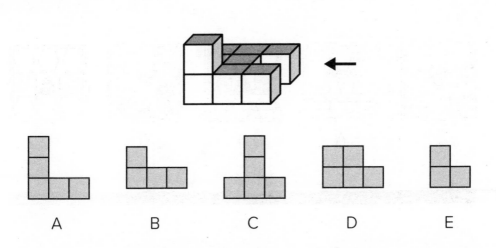

A   B   C   D   E

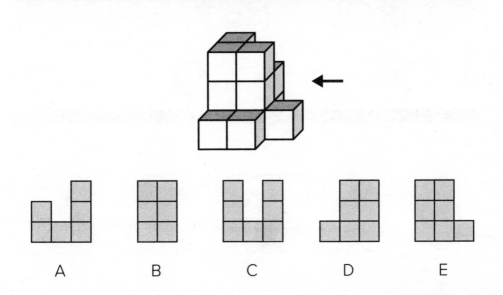

A   B   C   D   E

VISUAL
THINKING

FIND THE RULE

Based on the given example transformations, which of the options from A to E should replace the question mark symbol?

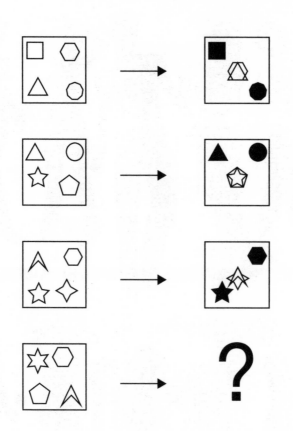

A   B   C   D   E

VISUAL THINKING

SPOT THE CHANGES

Can you find the five differences between the two images?

BUILDING BLOCKS

Which of the sets of blocks, A to D, can be rearranged to form the assembly shown? All blocks must be used exactly once each.

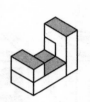

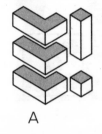

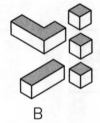

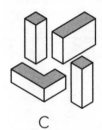

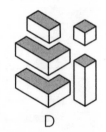

A   B   C   D

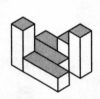

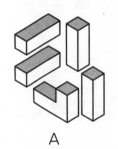

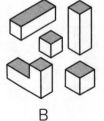

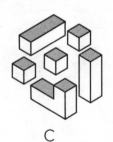

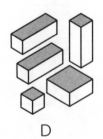

A   B   C   D

VISUAL THINKING

Which of the options, A to E, should replace the blank face on the cube so that they all become different views of the same cube? The correct face may need rotating.

A   B   C   D   E

A   B   C   D   E

HIDDEN IMAGE

Which of the options, A to D, conceals the image shown on the far left of each row? It may be rotated but all elements of it must be visible.

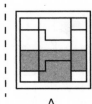

A B C D

 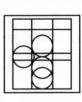

A B C D

 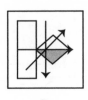 

A B C D

VISUAL THINKING

Which of the options, A to E, represents the view of the 3D object when seen from the direction of the arrow?

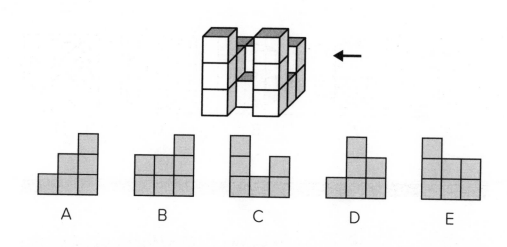

A   B   C   D   E

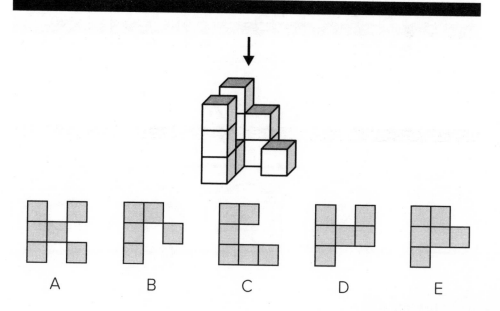

A   B   C   D   E

VISUAL THINKING

UPON REFLECTION

Which of the options, A to E, would result when each image is reflected in the dashed line shown?

A   B   C   D   E

A   B   C   D   E

COLOUR BY SHAPE

52

Colour each shape according to the key, to reveal a colourful hidden picture.

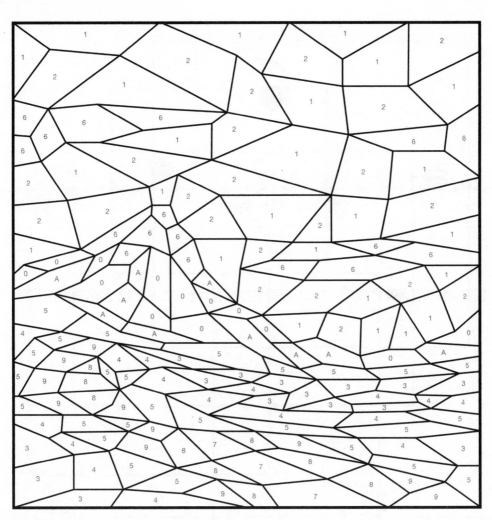

1 – light blue

2 – blue

3 – light green

4 – green

5 – dark green

6 – white

7 – light brown

8 – brown

9 – dark brown

0 – light grey

A – grey

VISUAL THINKING

SHAPE COUNTING

How many squares and/or rectangles can you count in this image? Many of them will overlap.

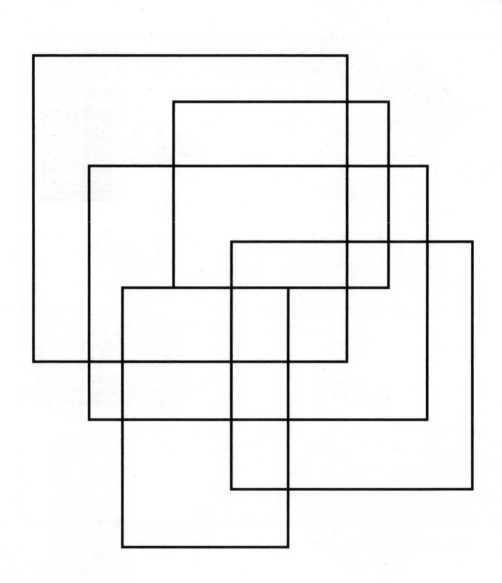

Join these DJs into identical pairs,
allowing for rotation.

SPOT THE CUBE

If you were to cut out and fold this image to make a six-sided cube, which of the cube images beneath, A to E, is the only one that could be formed?

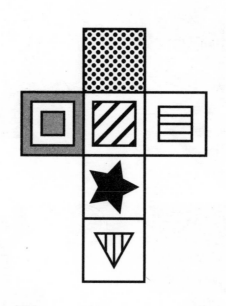

A

B

C

D

E

FIND THE PAIR

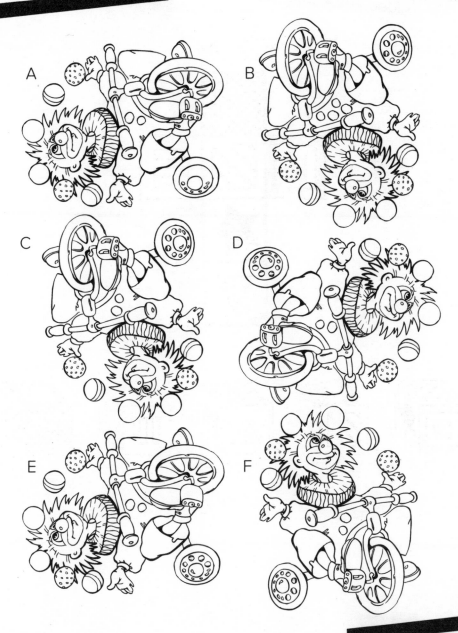

Which two of these images are identical, allowing for rotation?

A

B

C

D

E

F

VISUAL
THINKING

Join the dots with straight lines in increasing numerical order, starting at '1' (marked with a star), to reveal a hidden picture.

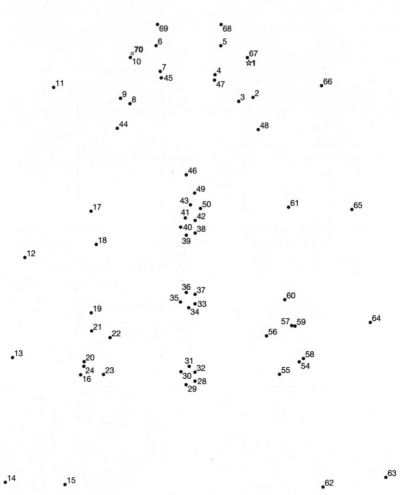

Which of the options, A to E, should be placed into the empty box in order to complete the pattern?

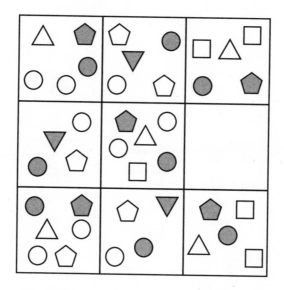

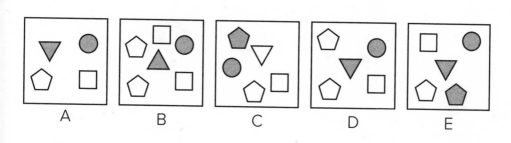

A   B   C   D   E

VISUAL THINKING

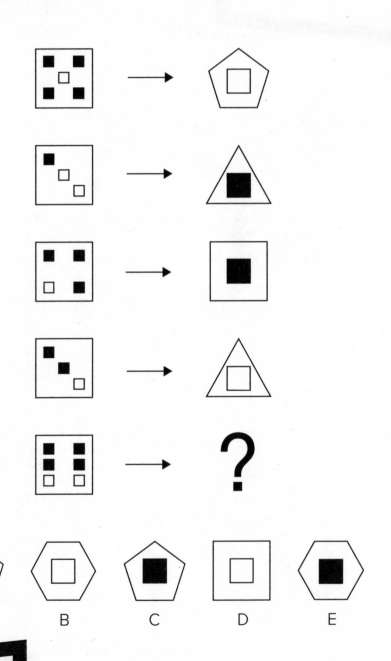

A B C D E

VISUAL THINKING

Can you find the five differences between the two images?

VISUAL
THINKING

If you were to cut out and fold this image to make a six-sided cube, which of the cube images beneath, A to E, could not be formed?

A

B

C

D

E

MATCHING HALVES

62

Join the eight halves together to make four complete strawberries.

A

B

C

D

E

F

G

H

RECTANGLE MAZE

Find your way through the maze.

Which option, from A to E, should replace the question mark symbols in order to continue each sequence?

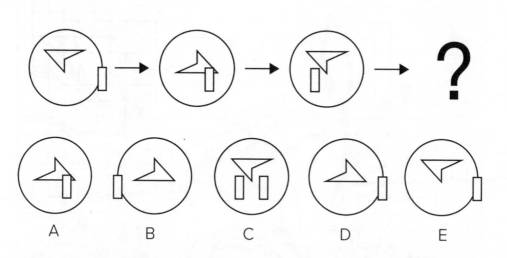

A   B   C   D   E

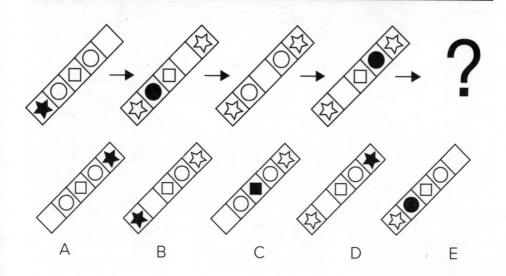

A   B   C   D   E

65

Which of the images, A to F, exactly matches a portion of the main image?

A
B
C

D

E

F

VISUAL THINKING

Which option, from A to E, should replace the question mark symbol? The rule applied on the left of the ':' should also be applied on the right.

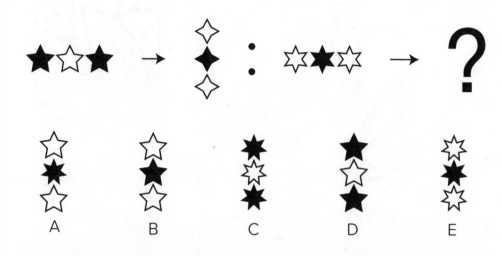

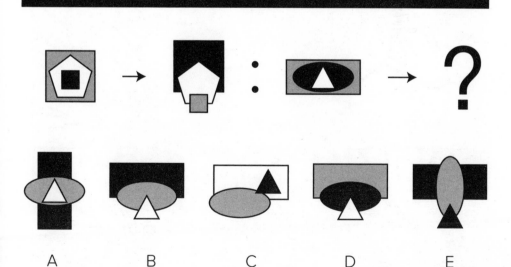

DOT TO DOT

Join the dots with straight lines in increasing numerical order, starting at '1' (marked with a star), to reveal a hidden picture.

PATTERN POSER

Which of the options, A to E, should be placed into the empty box in order to complete the pattern?

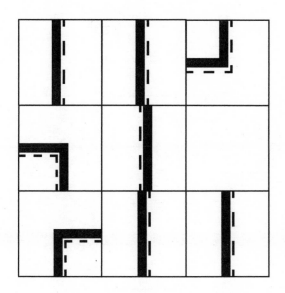

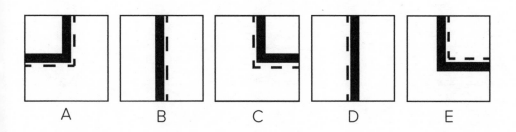

A   B   C   D   E

VISUAL
THINKING

TRACING PAPER

Which of the options, A to E, represents the view of the image shown at the top when folded in half along the dashed line? Assume it has been drawn on transparent paper.

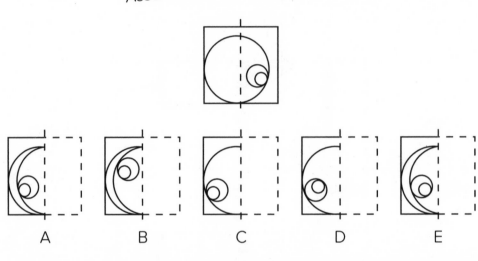

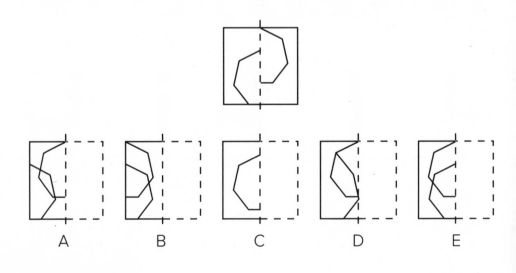

Which of the options, A to D, represents a view of the first 3D object when seen from the direction of the arrow?

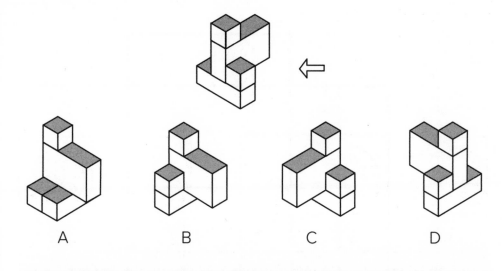

A   B   C   D

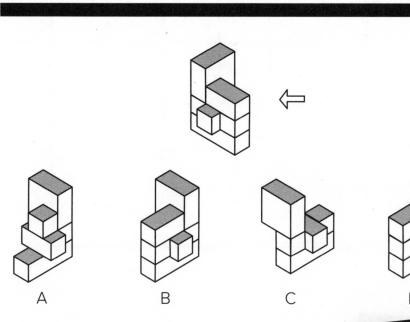

A   B   C   D

VISUAL THINKING

SHAPE COUNTING

How many squares and/or rectangles can you count in this image? Many of them will overlap.

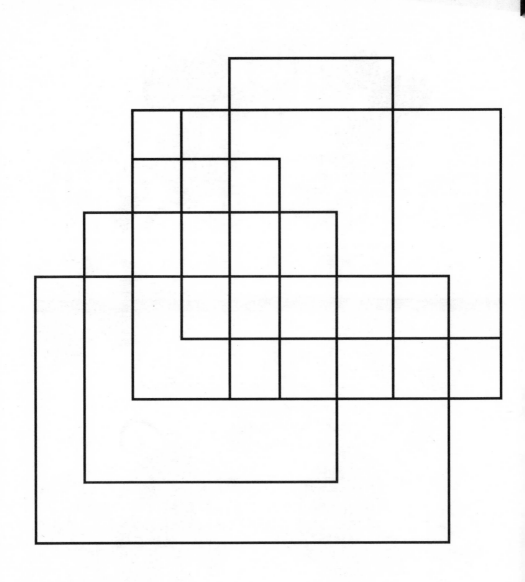

Join these bunches of flowers into identical pairs, allowing for rotation.

A

B

C

D

E

F

FIND THE RULE

Based on the given example transformations, which of the options from A to E should replace the question mark symbol?

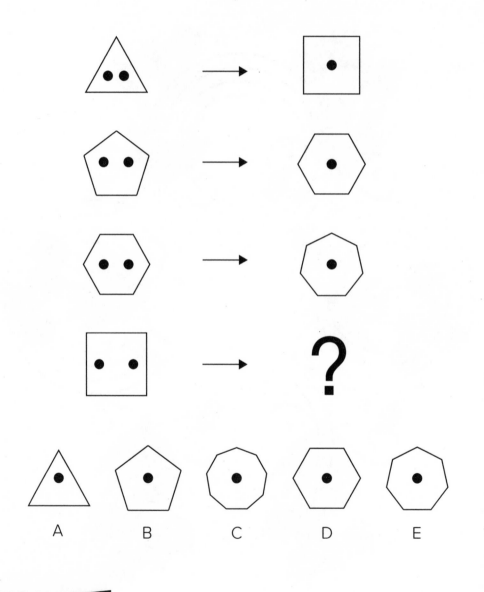

A　　B　　C　　D　　E

Use a ruler and a bold, dark marker to join the four dots to form a perfect straight-edged square. But what do you notice once this is drawn?

CUBIC CONUNDRUM

How many cubes are there in the following image? It began as a 5×5×5 block before some cubes were removed. None of the cubes are 'floating' in mid-air.

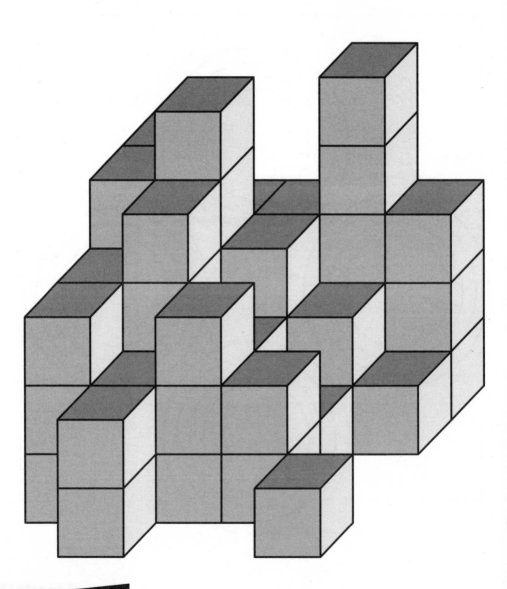

VISUAL THINKING

COLOUR BY PIXEL

Colour each square according to the key, to reveal a colourful hidden picture.

1	1	1	1	2	3	3	3	3	1	2	2	1	1	2	1	1	2	1	1
2	1	1	2	3	4	4	4	4	3	2	3	3	3	2	2	2	2	1	1
1	1	2	2	3	4	5	5	4	4	3	4	4	4	3	2	2	1	1	2
1	1	3	3	4	4	4	5	4	4	4	5	5	4	3	2	2	2	1	1
1	3	4	4	4	4	3	6	6	3	6	5	5	4	3	2	2	2	1	1
2	3	4	5	5	4	6	7	7	7	6	6	4	4	3	2	2	1	1	2
1	3	4	4	5	5	6	7	6	7	3	4	4	3	2	2	2	2	1	1
1	1	3	3	4	4	3	7	7	7	6	6	4	4	3	2	2	2	1	1
1	1	2	2	3	4	6	6	6	3	6	5	5	5	4	3	2	1	1	1
1	1	2	3	4	4	5	5	4	4	4	5	5	5	4	3	2	2	1	2
2	1	1	3	4	5	5	5	4	4	3	4	4	4	4	3	2	2	1	1
1	1	2	3	4	5	5	4	4	4	3	3	3	3	3	2	2	1	1	1
1	2	2	2	3	4	4	4	3	3	3	2	2	2	8	8	9	9	9	1
1	9	9	8	2	3	3	3	0	0	2	8	8	8	9	9	8	8	0	1
2	1	0	9	8	8	2	2	9	0	2	8	9	9	8	8	8	0	1	2
1	1	0	0	9	9	8	8	9	0	A	9	8	8	8	8	8	0	1	1
A	A	B	A	0	0	9	0	9	0	8	8	8	8	8	8	0	A	A	A
B	B	B	A	A	A	A	A	9	0	9	0	0	0	0	0	0	A	B	B
A	A	B	B	B	B	B	B	B	B	B	B	B	B	B	B	B	B	B	A
A	A	A	A	B	A	A	A	A	B	B	B	A	A	A	A	A	A	A	A

1 – blue	5 – light orange	9 – light green
2 – light blue	6 – orange	0 – dark green
3 – dark red	7 – yellow	A – brown
4 – red	8 – green	B – light brown

FIND THE RULE

Based on the given example transformations, which of the options from A to E should replace the question mark symbol?

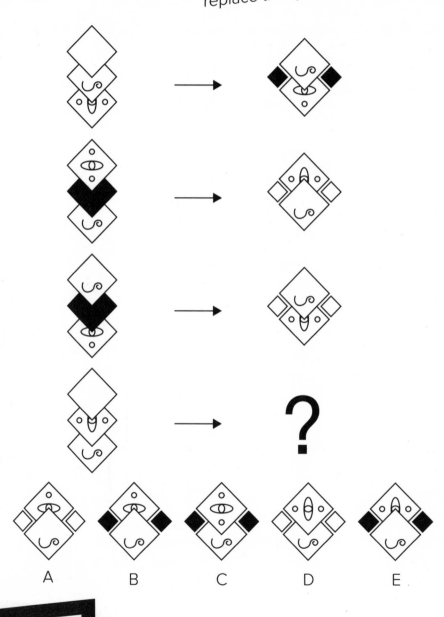

A B C D E

ILLUSORY IMAGE

Which of the three horizontal rectangles do you think is identical in size to the topmost, vertical rectangle? Check if you are correct.

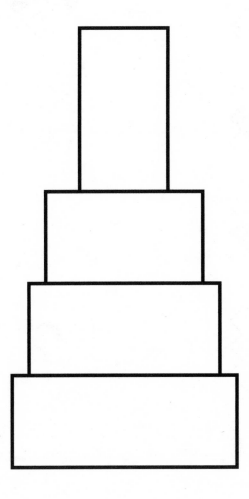

Join the dots with straight lines in increasing numerical order, starting at '1' (marked with a star), to reveal a hidden picture.

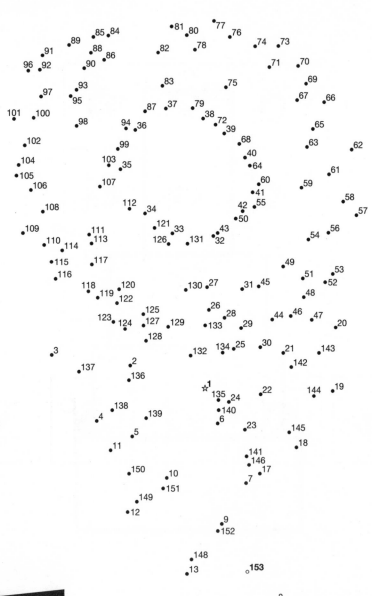

Which of the options, A to E, should be placed into the empty box in order to complete the pattern?

A   B   C   D   E

If you were to cut out and fold this image to make a six-sided cube, which of the cube images beneath, A to E, is the only one that could be formed?

A   B   C   D   E

VISUAL THINKING

FIND THE PAIR

Which two of these butterflies are identical, allowing for rotation?

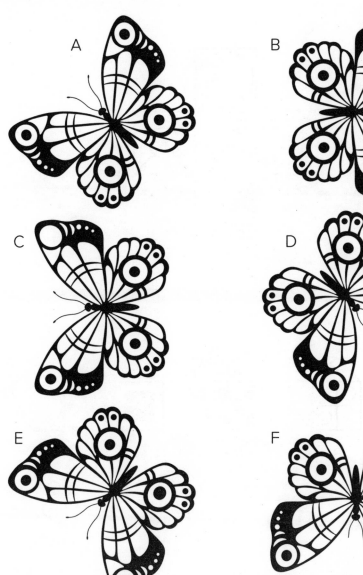

A

B

C

D

E

F

BUILDING BLOCKS

Which of the sets of blocks, A to D, can be rearranged to form the assembly shown? All blocks must be used exactly once each.

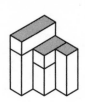

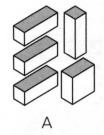

A

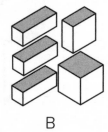

B

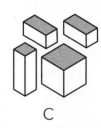

C

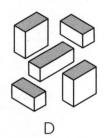

D

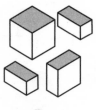

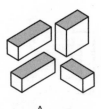

A

B

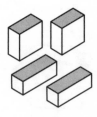

C

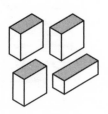

D

Which of the options, A to E, should replace the blank face on the cube so that they all become different views of the same cube? The correct face may need rotating.

A   B   C   D   E

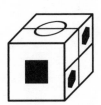 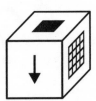

A   B   C   D   E

VISUAL THINKING

FIND THE RULE

Based on the given example transformations, which of the options from A to E should replace the question mark symbol?

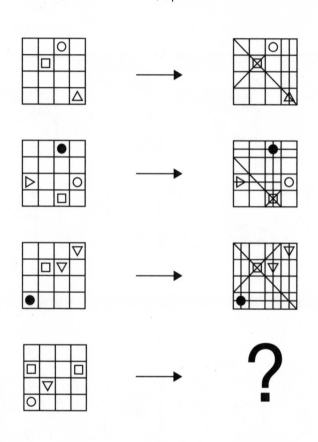

A

B

C

D

E

ILLUSORY IMAGE

Colour the grey squares a dark colour, such as black. Now draw bold, dark lines on the unbroken diagonals. What happens to these lines?

ODD ONE OUT

Which image is the odd one out on each line?

| A | B | C | D | E |

| A | B | C | D | E |

| A | B | C | D | E |

Which of the patterns, A to D, could be cut out and folded to match the view shown at the top?

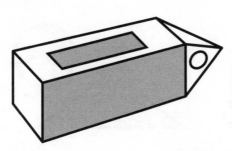

A

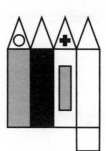

B

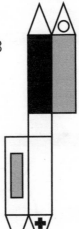

C

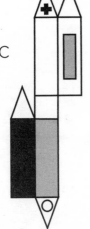

D

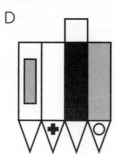

UPON ROTATION

Which of the options, A to E, is exactly the same as the first image of each puzzle, apart from its scale and the angle of its rotation?

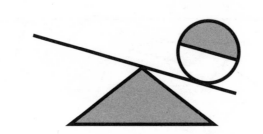

A   B   C   D   E

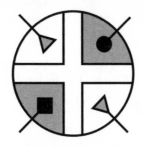

A   B   C   D   E

VISUAL THINKING

COLOUR BY SHAPE

Colour each shape according to the key, to reveal a colourful hidden picture.

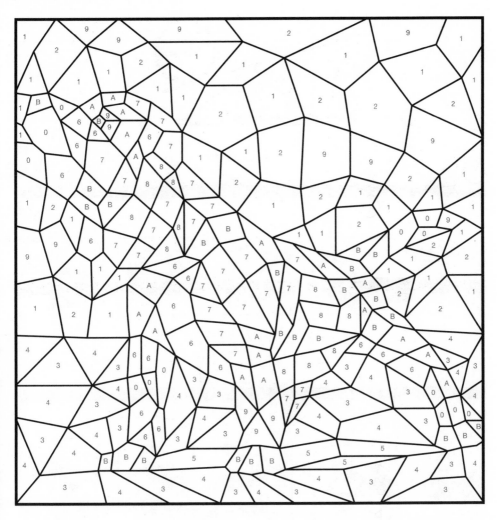

1 – pale blue

2 – light blue

3 – light green

4 – green

5 – dark green

6 – light brown

7 – brown

8 – dark brown

9 – white

0 – light grey

A – grey

B – dark grey

VISUAL THINKING

HIDDEN IMAGE

Which of the options, A to D, conceals the image shown on the far left of each row? It may be rotated but all elements of it must be visible.

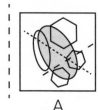 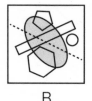 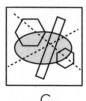 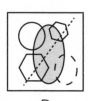

A   B   C   D

A   B   C   D

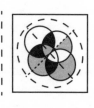 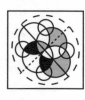 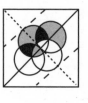

A   B   C   D

VISUAL THINKING

Which of the options, A to E, represents the view of the 3D object when seen from the direction of the arrow?

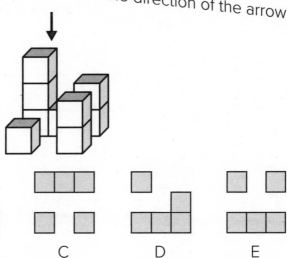

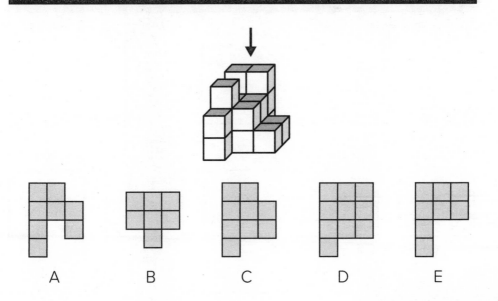

A   B   C   D   E

A   B   C   D   E

TRACING PAPER

Which of the options, A to E, represents the view of the image shown at the top when folded in half along the dashed line? Assume it has been drawn on transparent paper.

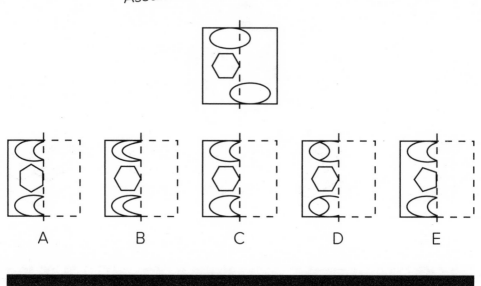

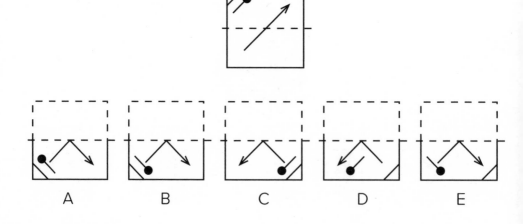

Which of the options, A to D, represents a view of the first 3D object when seen from the direction of the arrow?

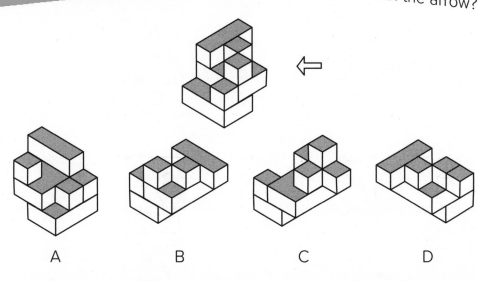

A   B   C   D

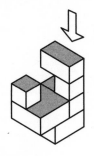

A   B   C   D

FIND THE RULE

Based on the given example transformations, which of the options from A to E should replace the question mark symbol?

 →

 →

 →

 → **?**

A   B   C   D   E

Compare the two central squares.
Which do you think is the larger?

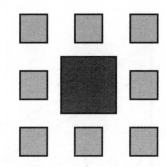

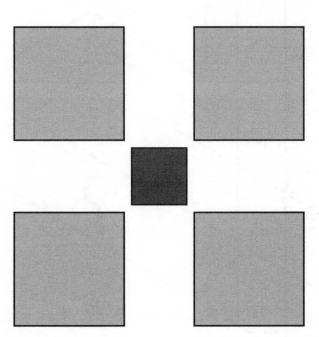

SHAPE COUNTING

How many triangles, including those formed via overlaps, can you count in this image?

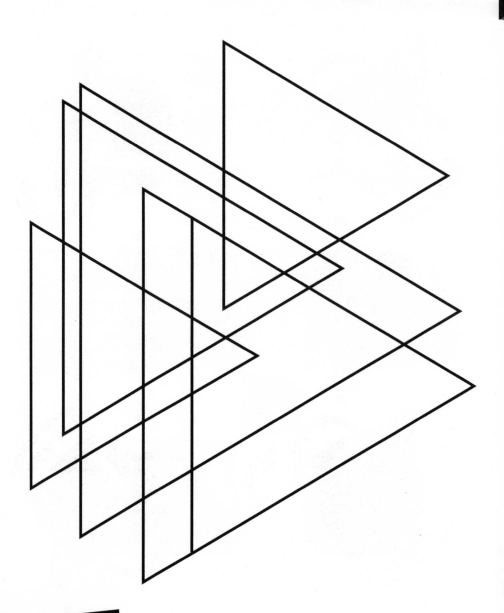

PAIRING PROBLEM

Join these cooking pots into identical pairs, allowing for rotation.

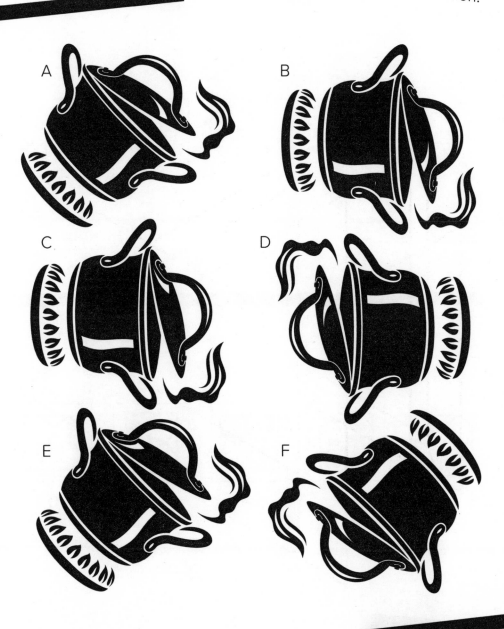

HIDDEN IMAGE

Which of the options, A to D, conceals the image shown on the far left of each row? It may be rotated but all elements of it must be visible.

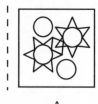
A

B

C

D

A

B

C

D

Which of the options, A to E, represents
the view of the 3D object when seen
from the direction of the arrow?

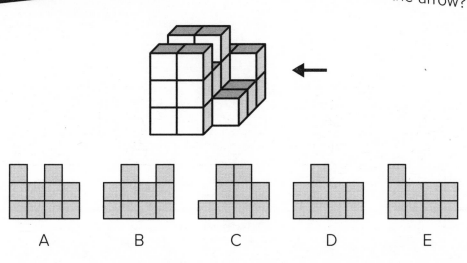

A   B   C   D   E

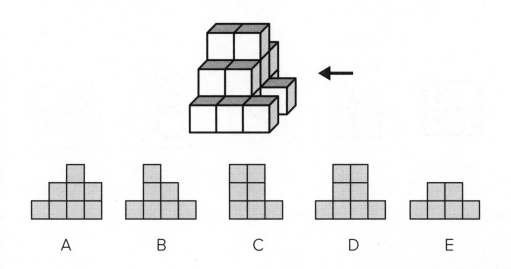

A   B   C   D   E

VISUAL THINKING

101

Join the dots with straight lines in increasing numerical order, starting at '1' (marked with a star), to reveal a hidden picture.

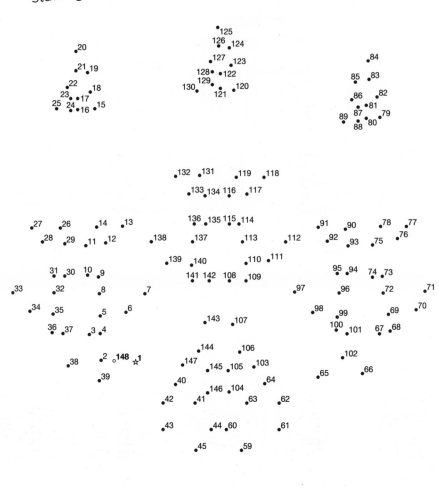

Which of the options, A to E, should be placed into the empty box in order to complete the pattern?

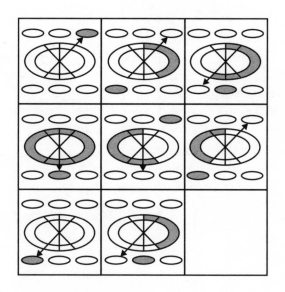

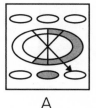
A

B

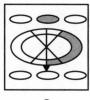
C

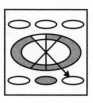
D

E

CUBIC CONUNDRUM

How many cubes are there in the following image? It began as a 5×5×5 block before some cubes were removed. None of the cubes are 'floating' in mid-air.

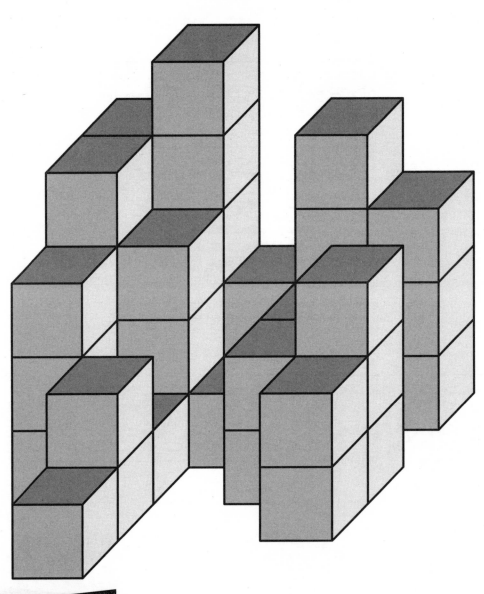

VISUAL THINKING

COLOUR BY PIXEL 104

Colour each square according to the key, to reveal a colourful hidden picture.

1	1	1	2	2	2	2	2	2	2	2	2	2	2	1	1	1	1	2
1	3	4	1	1	2	2	2	2	2	2	2	2	2	1	4	3	1	2
1	4	5	5	3	1	2	2	2	1	2	2	2	1	1	5	5	4	1	2
1	3	5	5	5	3	1	1	1	4	1	1	1	3	5	5	5	3	1	2
2	1	3	5	3	3	4	4	4	3	4	4	4	3	3	5	3	1	2	2
2	1	3	3	3	3	3	3	3	4	3	3	3	3	3	3	3	1	2	2
2	2	1	4	3	3	3	3	4	3	3	3	3	3	4	1	2	2	2
2	1	4	3	3	3	3	3	3	3	3	3	3	3	4	3	4	1	2	2
2	1	4	3	1	6	1	3	3	3	3	3	1	6	1	3	3	1	2	2
1	4	3	3	1	1	1	3	3	3	3	3	1	1	1	3	4	1	2
1	4	4	4	3	3	3	3	7	7	7	3	3	3	3	4	3	4	1	2
1	7	7	4	4	3	3	7	1	1	1	7	3	3	4	4	7	7	1	2
8	1	7	7	7	4	3	7	7	1	7	7	3	4	7	7	7	1	8	9
9	1	7	7	7	7	1	1	7	1	7	1	1	7	7	7	7	1	9	8
8	9	1	1	7	7	7	1	1	1	1	1	7	7	7	7	1	9	8	9
9	8	9	1	1	7	7	7	1	0	1	7	7	7	7	1	1	8	8	9
8	9	8	1	4	1	7	7	7	1	7	7	7	1	1	4	1	9	9	8
9	9	9	1	4	4	1	1	1	1	1	1	1	4	4	4	1	9	8	1
9	8	9	1	1	4	3	4	4	4	4	4	4	3	4	4	1	9	1	1
9	9	8	9	1	4	4	4	3	4	4	4	3	4	4	4	1	1	1	9

1 – black
2 – light blue
3 – orange
4 – brown
5 – dark orange
6 – blue
7 – white
8 – light green
9 – green
0 – pink

VISUAL THINKING

ANGULAR MAZE

Find your way through
the maze.

**VISUAL
THINKING**

Which option, from A to E, should replace the question mark symbols in order to continue each sequence?

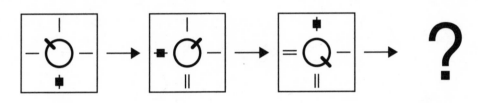

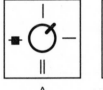

A   B   C   D   E

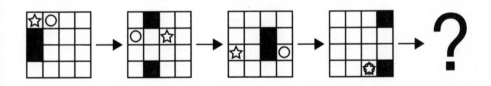

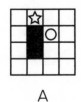

A   B   C   D   E

VISUAL THINKING

BUILDING BLOCKS

Which of the sets of blocks, A to D, can be rearranged to form the assembly shown? All blocks must be used exactly once each.

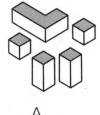 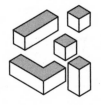 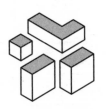 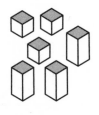

A   B   C   D

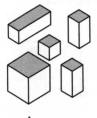 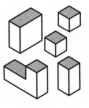 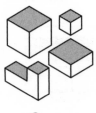 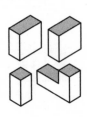

A   B   C   D

VISUAL THINKING

Which of the options, A to E, should replace the blank face on the cube so that they all become different views of the same cube? The correct face may need rotating.

A   B   C   D   E

A   B   C   D   E

VISUAL THINKING

UPON ROTATION

Which of the options, A to E, is exactly the same as the first image of each puzzle, apart from its scale and the angle of its rotation?

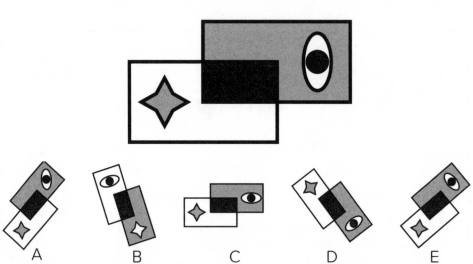

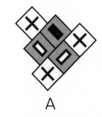 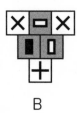  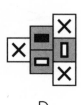 

A   B   C   D   E

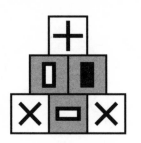

A   B   C   D   E

COLOUR BY SHAPE

Colour each shape according to the key, to reveal a colourful hidden picture.

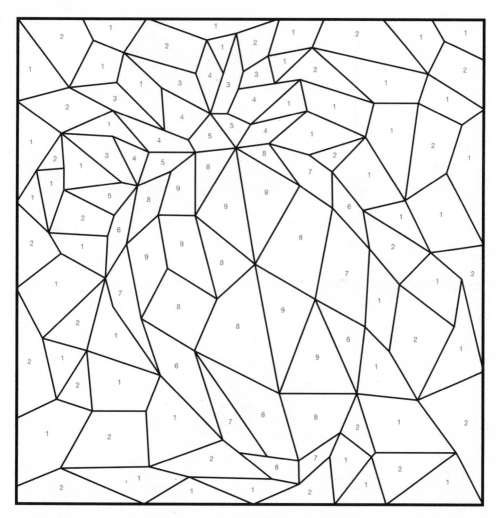

1 – light blue	5 – dark green	9 – dark red
2 – blue	6 – light orange	
3 – light green	7 – orange	
4 – green	8 – red	

VISUAL THINKING

111

Join the dots with straight lines in increasing numerical order, starting at '1' (marked with a star), to reveal a hidden picture.

Which of the options, A to E, should be placed into the empty box in order to complete the pattern?

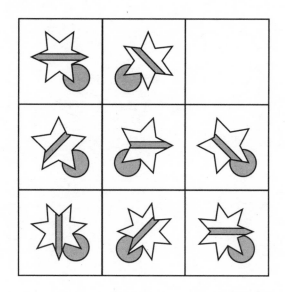

A

B

C

D

E

WAVY MAZE

Find your way through
the maze.

Which option, from A to E, should replace the question mark symbols in order to continue each sequence?

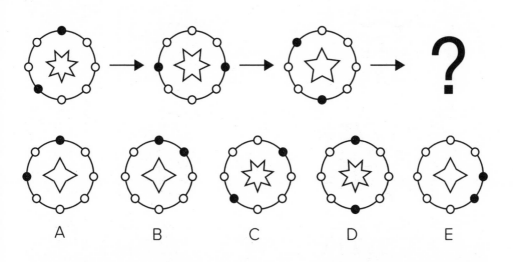

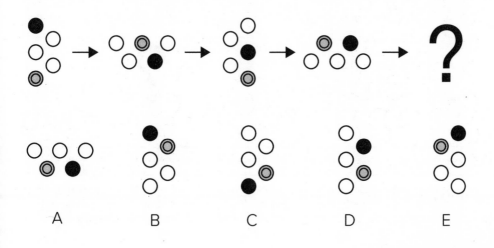

Based on the given example transformations, which of the options from A to E should replace the question mark symbol?

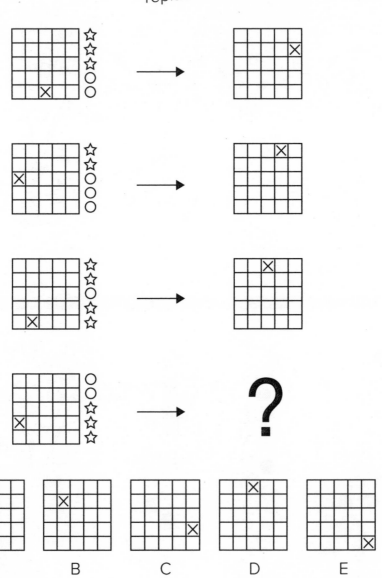

A B C D E

SPOT THE CHANGES 116

Can you find the five differences
between the two images?

UPON ROTATION

Which of the options, A to E, is exactly the same as the first image of each puzzle, apart from its scale and the angle of its rotation?

A

B

C

D

E

A

B

C

D

E

VISUAL THINKING

COLOUR BY SHAPE

Colour each shape according to the key, to reveal a colourful hidden picture.

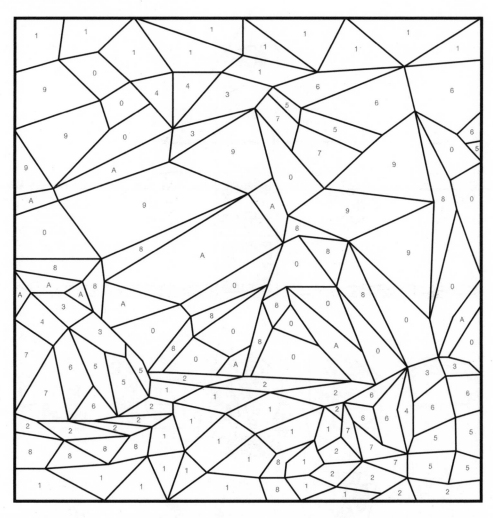

1 – light blue   5 – light brown   9 – light grey

2 – dark blue   6 – brown   0 – grey

3 – light green   7 – dark brown   A – dark grey

4 – green   8 – white

VISUAL THINKING

INCORRECT CUBE

If you were to cut out and fold this image to make a six-sided cube, which of the cube images beneath, A to E, could not be formed?

A

B

C

D

E

MATCHING HALVES 120

Join the eight halves together to
make four complete lion heads.

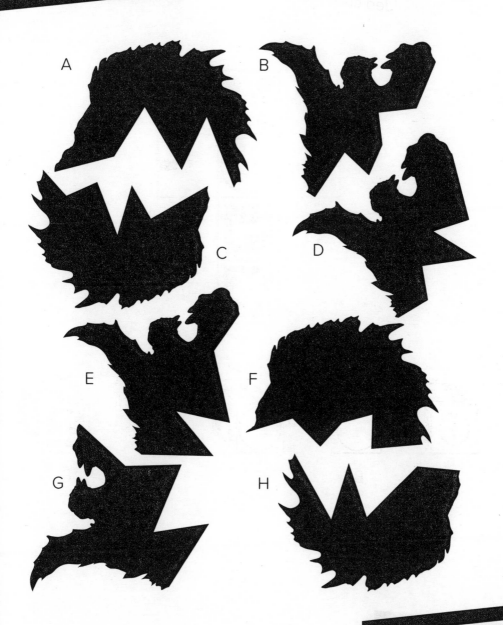

121

Join the dots with straight lines in increasing numerical order, starting at '1' (marked with a star), to reveal a hidden picture.

VISUAL
THINKING

Which of the options, A to E, should be placed into the empty box in order to complete the pattern?

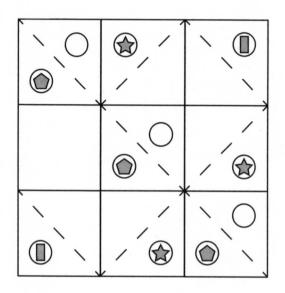

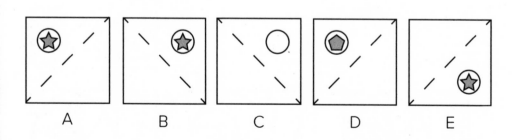

A   B   C   D   E

ROSY RECKONING

Which of the images, A to F, exactly matches a portion of the main image?

A

B

C

D

E

F

TRANSFORM AGAIN 124

Which option, from A to E, should replace the question mark symbol? The rule applied on the left of the ':' should also be applied on the right.

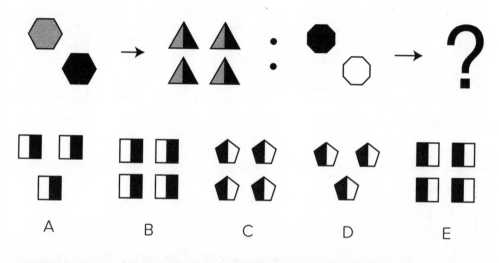

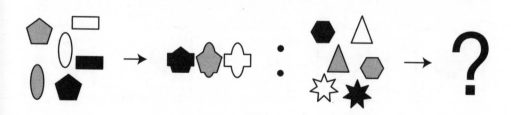

A   B   C   D   E

A   B   C   D   E

CRACK THE CODE

Crack the code used to describe each image, and circle the correct identifier for the image on the second line of each puzzle.

HIM   LWK   HIK   LJM   HWM

 = LJK   LWM   HIL   LIK   IMK

CD   YQ   YD   CN   YN

 = CQ   DN   DC   NC   CY

Which of the options, A to E, is an exact mirror image of the lion?

A

B

Original
image

C

D

E

WAVY MAZE

Find your way through the maze.

Which option, from A to E, should replace the question mark symbols in order to continue each sequence?

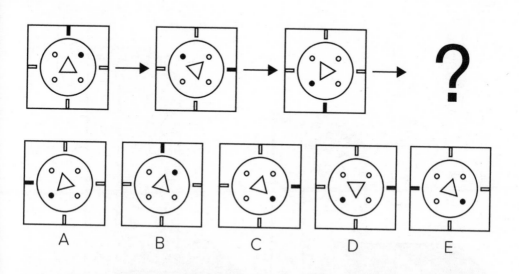

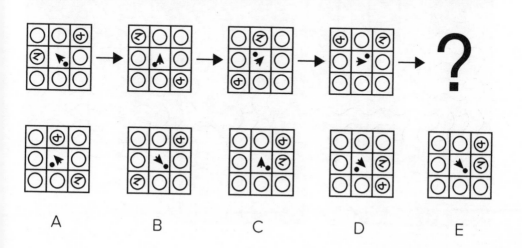

129 CUBIC CONUNDRUM

How many cubes are there in the following image? It began as a 5×5×5 block before some cubes were removed. None of the cubes are 'floating' in mid-air.

COLOUR BY PIXEL

Colour each square according to the key, to reveal a colourful hidden picture.

1	1	1	2	2	3	2	2	2	4	4	4	5	5	4	4	4	2	2	2
1	1	2	2	3	3	2	2	4	6	6	7	4	5	5	5	7	4	2	2
1	2	2	2	2	2	2	2	5	5	6	5	6	6	6	5	5	6	2	2
2	2	2	2	2	2	2	4	4	7	5	5	6	5	5	5	5	5	5	2
2	2	3	3	3	2	4	4	6	6	6	5	5	7	5	8	5	6	7	5
2	3	3	2	2	2	2	6	7	5	8	8	5	5	8	8	5	5	6	6
2	2	2	2	2	2	2	2	2	5	5	8	8	8	5	5	7	5	5	5
2	2	2	2	2	2	2	2	2	2	5	5	8	9	8	2	5	2	2	2
2	2	2	2	3	3	2	3	2	2	2	2	8	9	8	2	2	2	2	2
2	2	2	3	3	2	2	2	2	2	2	8	9	9	8	2	2	2	3	3
2	2	2	2	2	2	2	2	2	2	2	8	9	9	8	2	2	3	3	2
2	2	2	2	2	2	2	2	2	2	2	8	9	8	2	2	2	2	2	2
2	2	2	2	2	2	2	2	2	2	2	2	8	9	8	2	2	2	2	2
2	2	2	2	2	2	2	2	2	2	2	2	8	8	8	2	2	2	2	2
0	0	0	0	0	0	0	4	4	4	4	4	6	6	6	6	6	6	6	6
6	0	0	3	3	0	0	0	0	4	4	5	6	5	6	6	5	6	5	6
6	5	0	0	0	0	3	0	0	0	0	0	5	5	5	5	6	5	6	6
5	5	8	9	5	0	0	0	3	0	3	0	0	0	0	5	9	9	8	8
5	6	5	5	9	8	9	8	0	0	0	3	0	0	0	0	0	8	9	9
5	5	6	6	5	5	8	8	9	8	0	0	0	0	0	0	3	3	0	0
6	5	6	5	6	5	5	6	5	8	8	8	8	0	0	0	0	0	3	0

1 – yellow

2 – light blue

3 – light grey

4 – light green

5 – dark green

6 – green

7 – red

8 – brown

9 – light brown

0 – blue

VISUAL THINKING

If you were to cut out and fold this image to make a six-sided cube, which of the cube images beneath, A to E, is the only one that could be formed?

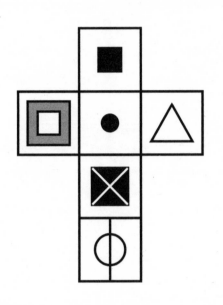

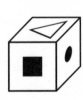

A   B   C   D   E

Which two of these ballerinas are identical, allowing for rotation?

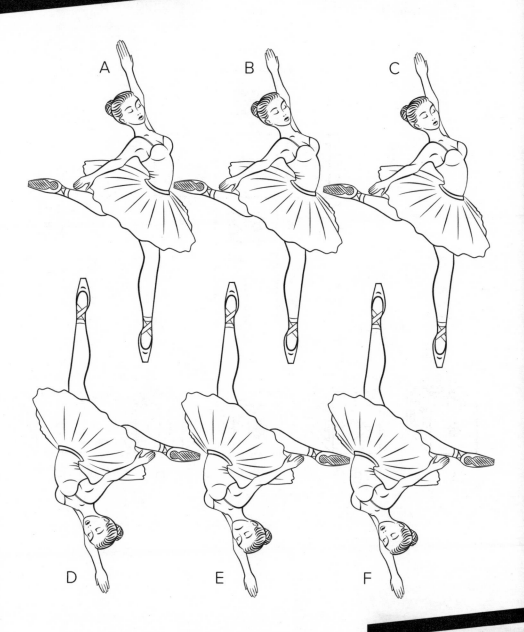

A　　B　　C

D　　E　　F

DOT TO DOT

Join the dots with straight lines in increasing numerical order, starting at '1' (marked with a star), to reveal a hidden picture.

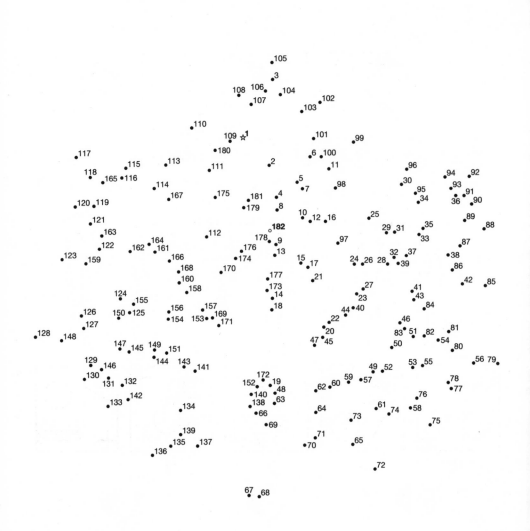

PATTERN POSER

Which of the options, A to E, should be placed into the empty box in order to complete the pattern?

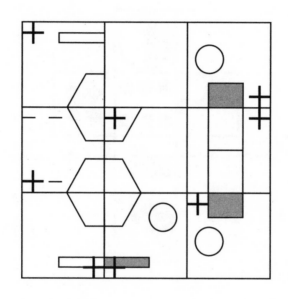

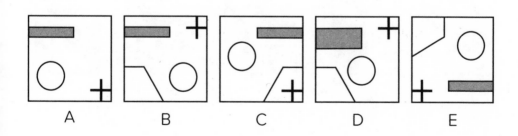

A   B   C   D   E

VISUAL THINKING

INCORRECT CUBE

If you were to cut out and fold this image to make a six-sided cube, which of the cube images beneath, A to E, could not be formed?

A   B   C   D   E

VISUAL THINKING

MATCHING HALVES

Join the eight halves together to make four complete flowers.

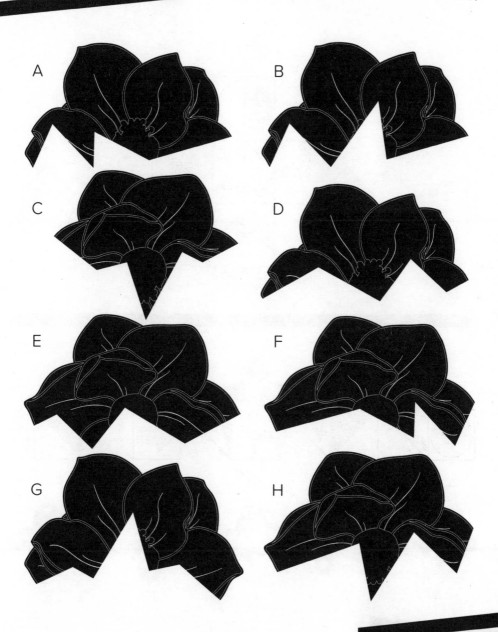

A

B

C

D

E

F

G

H

UPON REFLECTION

Which of the options, A to E, would result when each image is reflected in the dashed line shown?

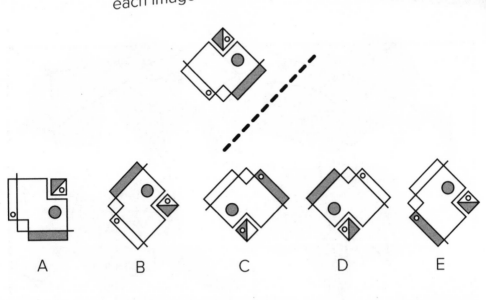

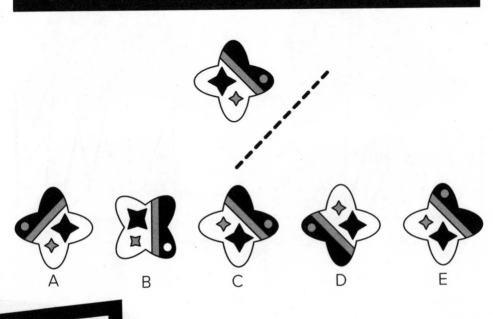

COLOUR BY SHAPE

Colour each shape according to the key, to reveal a colourful hidden picture.

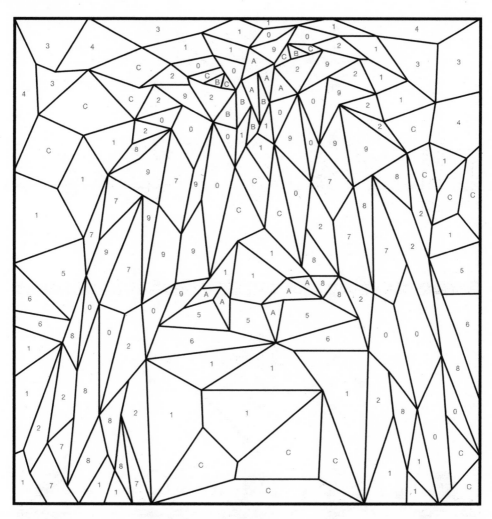

1 – pale blue   5 – light brown   9 – dark orange   C – white

2 – blue   6 – brown   0 – red

3 – light green   7 – yellow   A – dark grey

4 – green   8 – orange   B – black

VISUAL THINKING

Based on the given example transformations,
which of the options from A to E should
replace the question mark symbol?

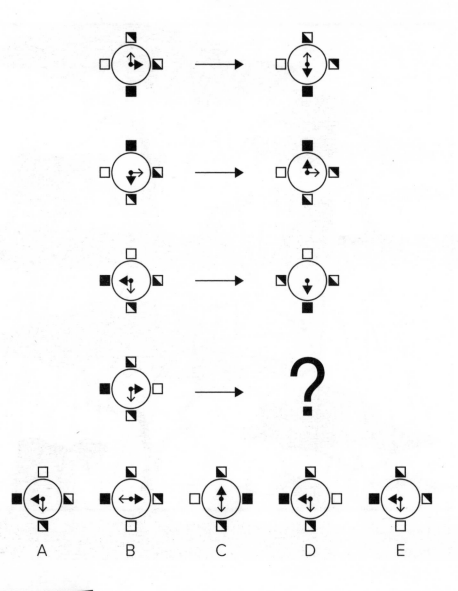

A   B   C   D   E

VISUAL THINKING

WHAT'S CHANGED? 140

Can you find the five differences between the two images?

141 CUBIC CONUNDRUM

How many cubes are there in the following image? It began as a 6×6×6 block before some cubes were removed. None of the cubes are 'floating' in mid-air.

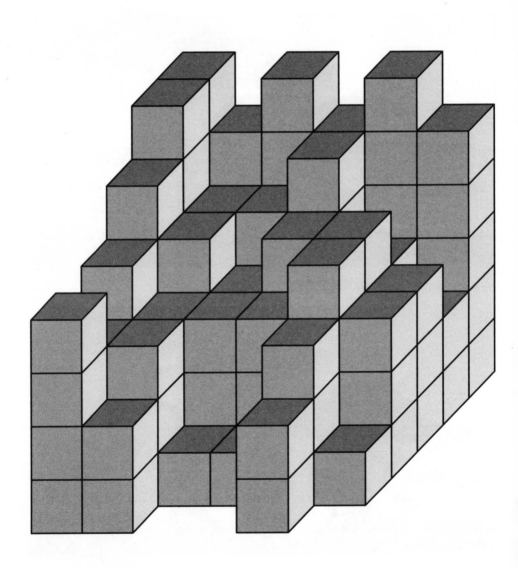

COLOUR BY PIXEL 142

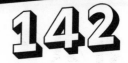

Colour each square according to the key, to reveal a colourful hidden picture.

1	1	1	1	1	1	2	2	1	1	1	1	2	2	1	1	1	1	1	2
1	2	1	1	1	1	2	2	2	3	1	1	3	2	3	1	1	1	2	3
2	3	2	4	1	1	2	3	2	2	1	4	2	3	2	1	1	1	3	2
2	3	5	6	4	6	7	3	8	5	4	6	8	3	7	1	4	4	2	8
3	2	2	6	4	6	3	7	3	5	4	6	7	3	5	6	6	4	7	3
3	7	2	6	4	6	7	8	3	3	4	6	3	8	5	6	4	6	7	5
7	5	5	4	6	6	7	7	7	5	4	6	3	7	5	6	6	6	7	7
7	8	3	4	6	6	7	3	8	5	6	6	3	7	7	6	6	6	7	3
7	5	5	4	6	6	7	3	5	5	6	6	7	7	7	6	6	6	7	3
8	5	2	4	6	6	7	3	3	5	6	6	7	5	7	6	4	6	7	5
7	5	7	6	6	6	7	7	3	5	6	6	5	5	7	6	6	6	7	5
7	5	7	6	4	6	7	7	5	7	6	6	5	7	7	4	6	6	7	7
7	7	5	6	4	6	7	5	5	7	6	6	5	7	7	4	6	6	7	5
7	7	5	6	6	6	7	5	5	5	6	6	5	5	7	6	6	6	7	5
7	5	5	6	6	6	7	5	7	5	6	6	5	5	5	6	4	6	7	7
7	5	5	6	4	6	7	5	7	7	6	4	7	7	5	6	4	4	7	4
8	7	7	4	4	6	7	7	7	7	4	4	7	7	4	4	4	4	4	4
7	8	4	4	4	4	7	7	4	4	4	4	4	4	4	4	4	4	1	1
4	4	4	1	1	4	4	4	4	4	4	4	4	1	1	1	1	1	1	1
1	1	1	1	1	1	1	1	1	1	1	1	1	1	1	1	1	1	1	1

1 – light blue
2 – light green
3 – green
4 – white

5 – dark green
6 – blue
7 – dark grey
8 – brown

VISUAL THINKING

Join the dots with straight lines in increasing numerical order, starting at '1' (marked with a star), to reveal a hidden picture.

PATTERN POSER

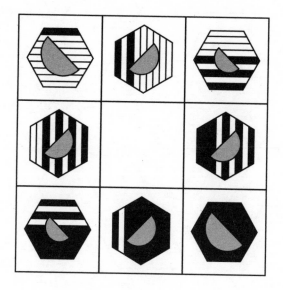

144

Which of the options, A to E, should be placed into the empty box in order to complete the pattern?

A   B   C   D   E

ANGULAR MAZE

Find your way through
the maze.

Which option, from A to E, should replace the question mark symbols in order to continue each sequence?

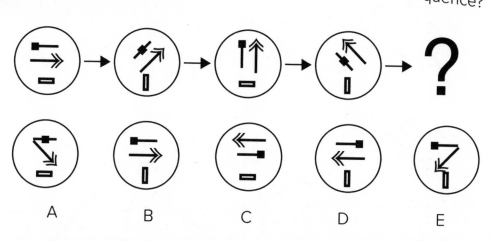

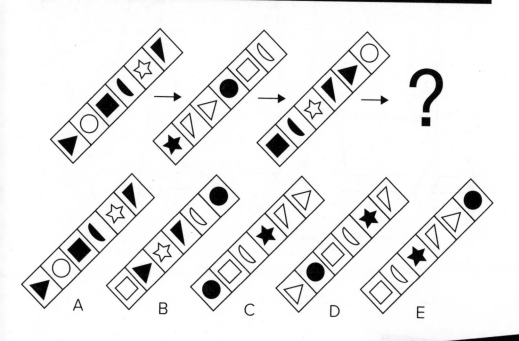

How many triangles, including those formed via overlaps, can you count in this image?

PAIRING PROBLEM 148

Join these cycling images into identical pairs.

A

B

C

D

E

F

ODD ONE OUT

Which image is the odd one out on each line?

A   B   C   D   E

A   B   C   D   E

A   B   C   D   E

VISUAL THINKING

Which of the patterns, A to D, could be cut out and folded to match the view shown at the top?

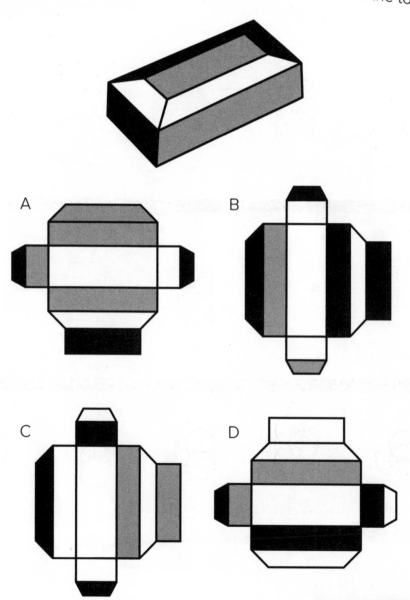

A

B

C

D

CUBIC CONUNDRUM

How many cubes are there in the following image? It began as a 6×6×6 block before some cubes were removed. None of the cubes are 'floating' in mid-air.

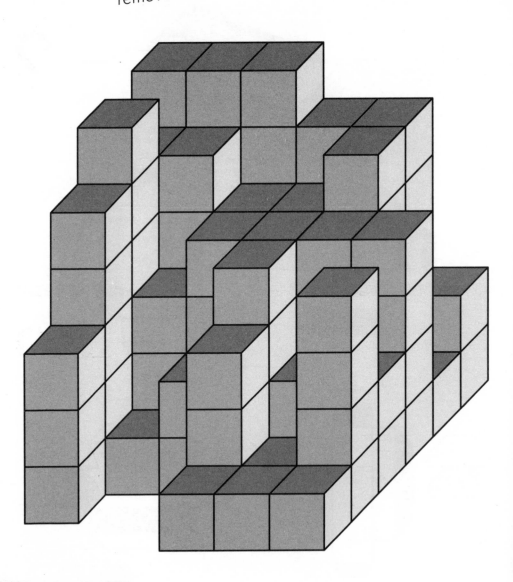

Which option, from A to E, should replace the question mark symbol? The rule applied on the left of the ':' should also be applied on the right.

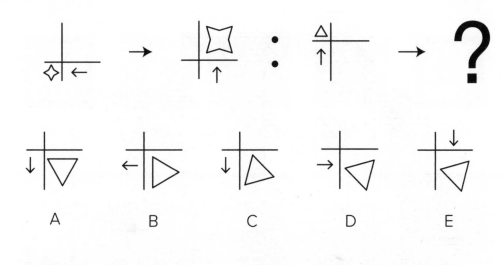

A   B   C   D   E

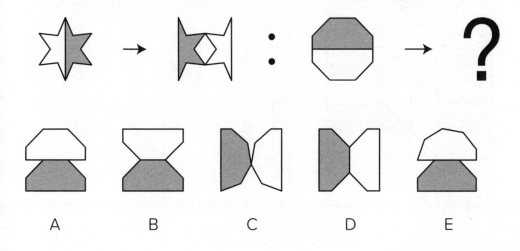

A   B   C   D   E

VISUAL THINKING

CRACK THE CODE

Crack the code used to describe each image, and circle the correct identifier for the image on the second line of each puzzle.

LFR

ESR

NBY

EFY

LUY

 EUY   LBR   NSR   NFR   LSY

QCA

NZK

NPA

SZK

SCK

= NPK   SZK   NZA   QCK   QZA

Which of the options, A to E, is an exact mirror image of the eagle?

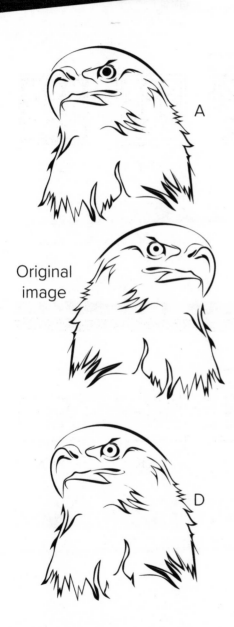

Original image

155

Which of the options, A to E, represents the view of the image shown at the top when folded in half along the dashed line? Assume it has been drawn on transparent paper.

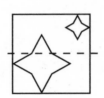

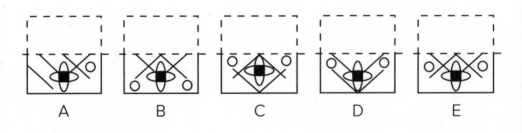

A   B   C   D   E

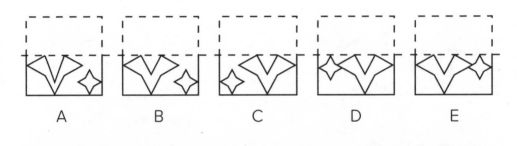

A   B   C   D   E

VISUAL THINKING

Which of the options, A to D, represents a view of the first 3D object when seen from the direction of the arrow?

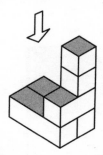

A

B

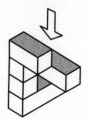

C

D

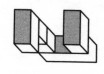

A

B

C

D

CUBIC CONUNDRUM

How many cubes are there in the following image? It began as a 6×6×6 block before some cubes were removed. None of the cubes are 'floating' in mid-air.

VISUAL THINKING

Which option, from A to E, should replace the question mark symbol? The rule applied on the left of the ':' should also be applied on the right.

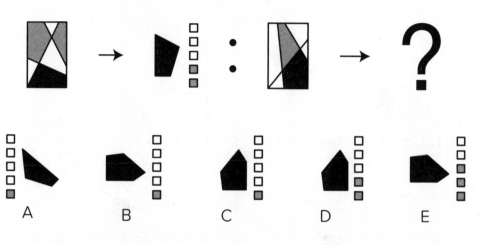

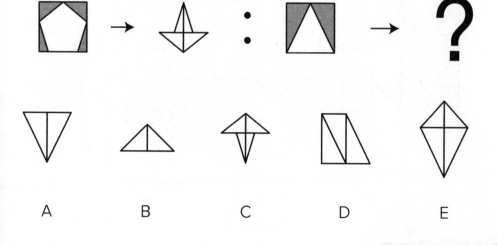

PATTERN POSER

Which of the options, A to D, should be placed into the empty triangle in order to complete the pattern?

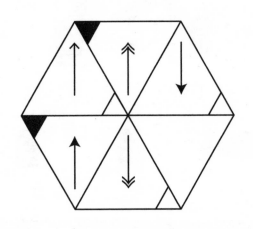

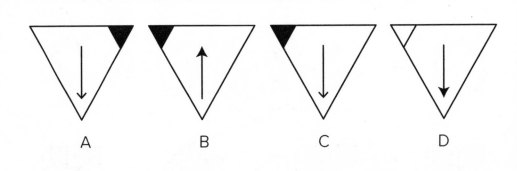

A   B   C   D

Which of the options, A to D, represents a view of the first 3D object when seen from the direction of the arrow?

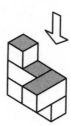

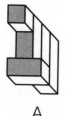

A

B

C

D

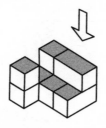

A

B

C

D

1
57 squares and rectangles

2
A-F, B-D, C-E

3
45 cubes

4
Hamburger:

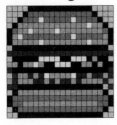

5
B

6
C

A

7
VS – The first letter refers to the colour of the rectangles (V = black, P = white). The second letter refers to the orientation of the rectangles (B = horizontal, S = vertical, N = diagonal).

URO – The first letter is the type of shape behind the star (U = circle, A = square, T = pentagon); the second letter is the colour of the star (R = grey, M = white); the third letter is the colour of the background shape (E = black, O = white).

8
C

9
Sailing boat:

SOLUTIONS

10

D – The stars form a sequence reading from left to right and top to bottom. At each step, the star rotates 45 degrees anticlockwise. The shape in the corner of each square moves around the four corners in a clockwise direction, moving one corner at each step.

11

D – This is the only shape with an arrow pointing at a star rather than away from a star.

A – The other grey bars contain one less circle than the number of corners on their associated polygon.

E – This is the only shape with a clockwise spiral.

12

A

13

C

14

D
B

15

16

A - One point is added to the star and one side is added to the inner polygon at each step.

A - One triangle remains in place, while the second triangle rotates by 45 degrees clockwise at each step using the bottom-left corner of the stationary triangle as the point to rotate around. Each triangle has one circle attached, and each circle moves in a clockwise direction around its triangle, jumping from corner to corner.

17

A – Its top and side faces have been swapped.

18

A-C, B-H, D-F, E-G

19

D

20

A
B

21

66 squares and rectangles

22

A-D, B-E, C-F

23

Butterfly:

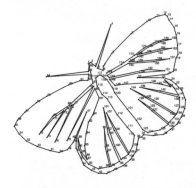

24

A – The squares form a sequence, reading from left to right and top to bottom. The sequence alternates between reflecting the image vertically and rotating

SOLUTIONS

it by 180 degrees, starting with reflection at the first step. When the image is reflected, one grey dot is added. When the image is rotated, one black dot is added.

25

C – This is the only square containing six areas rather than five.

E – This is the only grid containing smaller polygons with a total number of corners that does not equal 15.

C – This is the only image which features a polygon where not all sides are the same length.

26

C

27

UFL – The first letter is the type of white shape (O = star, R = triangle, U = oval); the second letter is the colour of the square (G = black, E = grey, F = white); the third letter is the location of the square (L = within the shape indicated by letter 1, B = outside of the shape indicated by letter 1).

EJH – The first letter is the orientation of the shape (E = rotated squares above non-rotated squares, N = rotated squares below non-rotated squares, S = rotated squares to the left of non-rotated squares, O = rotated squares to the right of non-rotated squares); the second letter is whether the line going through the rotated squares is dotted or solid (C = dotted, J = solid); the final letter is how many points are on the star (X = 5, H = 6).

28

B

29

E – A has an incorrect top
face; B has its front and side
faces swapped; C has its
top face rotated incorrectly;
D has a face that does not
appear on the cube net.

30

B and F

31

C
A
D

32

A
D

33

34 cubes

34

The Earth:

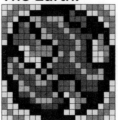

35

D
B

36

A
C

37

B
D

38

Apple tree:

39

A:

B:

40

E

D

41

A

42

D

E

43

B

C

D

44

B

D

45

C – Each of the left-hand boxes contains one smaller shape which has exactly double the number of sides to another small shape

A:

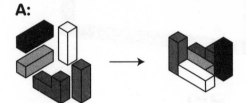

located in the same box.
These two shapes snap
together in the centre of
the right-hand box, and the
two remaining shapes are
shaded black.

48

B

D

46

49

C

A

B

50

E

B

47

D:

51

C

D

SOLUTIONS

56

C and D

52

Mountain landscape:

57

Coat:

53

43 squares and rectangles

54

A-F, B-C, D-E

55

A – B has its front and side faces swapped; C has an incorrect side face; D has its front and side faces swapped; E has a face that does not appear on the cube net.

58

D – Each row and column has a total of nine white shapes. There are also two shaded shapes in each square, one of which is a circle and the other of which is either a pentagon or a triangle on a chequerboard pattern.

VISUAL THINKING

59

B – The number of small squares in the left-hand box matches the number of sides of the outer shape on the right-hand side. If an odd number of small squares in the left-hand box is shaded black, then the central square on the right-hand side will be shaded black; if an even number is shaded black, then the central square on the right-hand side will be white.

60

61

C – Its front and side faces have been swapped.

62

A-H, B-E, C-F, D-G

63

B – The arrow shape within the circle rotates by 180 degrees at each step; the rectangle moves from right to left horizontally across the circle.

A – Shapes remain in the same order, but the empty square moves from right to left by one square per step, while the black shading moves one square right at each step.

F

D – The colours of the stars have been reversed, and the number of points on each star has been reduced by one. They have been rearranged to sit in a vertical rather than a horizontal line.

B – The three shapes have been spread out into a vertically aligned overlapping set with the largest shape at the top and the smallest at the bottom. The colours of the grey and black shapes have been switched.

Crab:

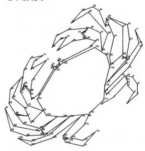

C – If you were to rotate each individual grid square by 90 degrees anticlockwise, the solid and dashed lines would join up to make a

73

B – One dot is removed from the centre of the left-hand shape; one side is added to the right-hand shape.

continuous path running between the boxes. The missing square is the one which would accurately complete this path if it was similarly rotated.

74

The square appears to bend:

69

A
E

70

B
D

71

121 squares and rectangles

75

56 cubes

72

A-D, B-E, C-F

76

Flower:

SOLUTIONS

77

B – The undecorated square from the left-hand shape changes colour to either black or white, and becomes two small squares at the left and right of the right-hand shape. The two remaining squares overlap in the centre of the right-hand shape, with the square featuring an eye design always sitting at the back. The square with an eye shape also rotates by 90 degrees.

78

Surprisingly, the topmost horizontal rectangle matches the vertical rectangle.

79

Daisy:

80

E – All of the shapes in the grid squares are a reflection of the shape in the central square, following either vertical, horizontal or diagonal mirror lines corresponding to the respective shape's position in the grid (for example the top right square is reflected along a line travelling diagonally from the central-top square to the rightmost square on the central row).

VISUAL THINKING

84

D

C

81

A – B has its front face rotated incorrectly; C has an incorrect front face; D has a face that does not appear on the cube net; E has its front and side faces swapped.

85

D – Each shape is transformed differently: squares are crossed by two perpendicular diagonal lines; black circles are crossed by a horizontal and a vertical line; triangles are bisected by a horizontal or vertical line through their most central point. All lines continue to the edge of the grid, except they do not enter squares containing white circles.

82

A and B

83

B:

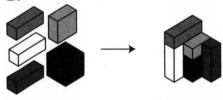

D:

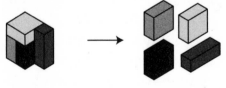

SOLUTIONS

86

The bold lines appear to bend, despite being parallel:

87

A – This is the only shape where the number of arrows does not match the number of sides of the polygon.

C – This is the only grid which does not have a row of three shaded squares forming one complete row or column.

B – This is the only image with just one grey shape.

88

D

89

B

C

90

Puppy:

91

A

D

C

92
C
C

93
C
B

94
B
A

95
C – The shape which is bisected by a line in the left-hand image becomes a larger shape which surrounds the circle in the right-hand image, and is also filled in black.

96
Both squares are the same size, despite the upper one appearing larger.

97
21 triangles

98
A-F, B-D, C-E

99
B
C

100
A
A

101
Candlestick holder:

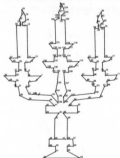

SOLUTIONS

104

Fox:

102

B – The small grey ovals are identical in each diagonal line from top left to bottom right, wrapping round the edges of the grid to form three separate diagonals. The remainder of each square forms a sequence, reading from left to right and top to bottom. Two adjacent areas of the large oval change colour at each step, working around the circle in a clockwise direction, changing between grey and white. At each step, the central arrow moves to point at the small oval which was shaded grey in the previous step.

105

106

B – The black square moves clockwise around the outer lines at each step. An extra black line is added in the position where the black square was positioned in the previous step. The

103

42 cubes

C:

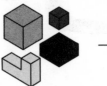

line which intersects the circle rotates in a clockwise direction, moving 90 degrees at each step.

B – The two shaded black squares move right by one column at each step, alternating between the central and edge squares. At each step, the star moves down one square and across two squares to the right. The circle moves down one square and across three squares to the right. If any shape would leave the grid, it 'wraps around' to the opposite end of the same row or column.

108

C
B

109

D
B

110

Strawberry:

107

A:

SOLUTIONS

position in each column and vertical position in each row.

111

Gecko:

113

112

E – Reading from left to right and top to bottom, the grey bar rotates 45 degrees clockwise at each step. The stars in the top row have six points, five in the middle row and seven in the bottom row. Within each row, the shape in the left-hand column rotates 90 degrees clockwise from the left to the central column, then is reflected vertically from the central to the right column. The grey circle stays in the same horizontal

114

A – The number of points on the star decreases by one at each step. The black dot which begins at the top of the circle moves clockwise by two positions around the circle, and the other black dot moves clockwise by one position, at each step.

C – The image rotates 90 degrees clockwise at each step. The black dot moves diagonally along the arrangement in a zigzag pattern, while the circle with another circle within it moves clockwise around the arrangement.

115

D – Each star to the right of the grid indicates that the cross should travel up one square, while each circle indicates it should travel right one square.

116

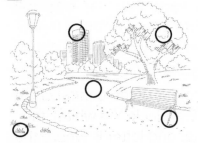

117

E

A

118

Stream between rocks:

119

B – Its front and side faces have been swapped.

120

A-G, B-F, C-D, E-H

121

High heels:

SOLUTIONS

122

A – The circles are in a symmetrical pattern across the whole grid, along the diagonal from the top-left to the bottom-right corner. The diagonal dashed lines switch diagonals at each step, reading along the grid squares from left to right and top to bottom. The grey shapes contained within the circles follow a pattern, reading in the same order: pentagon, blank, star, rectangle, star, then repeat.

123

E

124

E – Each shape is split into two identical shapes that together have the same total number of sides. The left of the new shapes is filled with the colour of the original left shape and the right with the colour of the original right shape.

C – Shapes with matching colours have been combined into a new shape, centring the two shapes together before combining.

125

LIK – The first letter is the orientation of the overall shape (H = corner in bottom left, L = corner in top right); the second letter is the colour of the corner square (W = black, I = white, J = grey); the third letter is the type of arrow head (K = solid, M = double lines).

CQ – The first letter is the colour of the central circle (C = black, Y = white); the second letter is where the circle is located (D = central, Q = top right, N = top left).

VISUAL THINKING

126
A

127

128

E – The black dot rotates around the circle in an anticlockwise direction, moving one position at each step. The black rectangle does the same, but moves in a clockwise direction. The central triangle rotates clockwise by 45 degrees at each step.

E – The central arrow rotates clockwise by 45 degrees at each step. The black dot moves between the four corners of the inner square in a clockwise direction. At each step the 'z' symbol moves clockwise by one outer circle and the 'twist' symbol moves clockwise by two outer circles.

129
35 cubes

130
Tree by river:

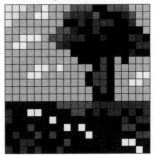

131

A – B has an incorrect side face; C has its top face rotated incorrectly; D has its front and side faces

SOLUTIONS

to corner in a clockwise direction, reading from left to right and top to bottom.

swapped; E has a face that does not appear on the cube net.

135

A – Its front and top faces have been swapped.

132

B and F

136

A-F, B-H, C-G, D-E

133

Maple leaf:

137

B

E

138

Parrots on a branch:

134

B – Apart from the bold crosses, the entire grid is symmetrical across the horizontal centre of the grid. At each step, the cross in the corner of the boxes moves from corner

VISUAL THINKING

139

E – The two arrows in each left-hand shape point to two squares, and these squares switch places in the right-hand shape. The arrow with a solid black head moves to point to the solid black square in the right-hand shape.

140

141

120 cubes

142

Waterfalls:

143

Clownfish:

144

C – The squares form a sequence, reading from left to right and top to bottom. The grey semicircle is reflected vertically at each step and changes size in the pattern large, medium, small, medium, large etc. One stripe of the hexagon

SOLUTIONS

is shaded black at each step, with alternate stripes being shaded until every other stripe is shaded, after which point the remaining stripes are filled in one at a time. The hexagon rotates by 90 degrees anticlockwise at each step.

145

146

C – The two lines rotate anticlockwise by 45 degrees at each step. The black square moves to the centre of the line after

the first step, then to the opposite end of the line, then back to the centre, then back to its starting position and so on. The rectangle at the bottom of the circle rotates by 90 degrees at each step.

D – Every shape changes colour from either black to white or white to black at each step. The shapes cycle positions, with every shape moving up two boxes at each step, moving into the bottom box when they cannot move any further up the grid.

147

27 triangles

148

A-C, B-F, D-E

149

D – This is the only shape made of two non-

overlapping shapes (and therefore the only one without two grey areas).

A – This is the only arrangement which does not feature a rotated square.

D – This is the only arrangement made of six circles rather than five.

150

C

151

109 cubes

152

D – The polygon in the smallest area moves to the largest area and is enlarged plus rotated 45 degrees. The arrow turns to point at the polygon.

B – The two differently shaded pieces swap places.

153

NSR – The first letter is the colour of the outlining box (L = black, E = white, N = grey); the second letter is the orientation of the lines in the circles (S = horizontal, U = vertical, F = top left to bottom right, B = top right to bottom left); the final letter is the colour of the central box (R = grey, Y = white).

QZA – The first letter defines which shape is shaded grey (Q = hexagon, N = rectangle, S = star); the second letter is which shape is at the front of the arrangement (P = hexagon, C = rectangle, Z = star); the final letter is the orientation of the rectangle (A = vertical, K = horizontal).

154

C

VISUAL THINKING

SOLUTIONS

155

B
E

156

B
D

157

74 cubes

158

B – The black shape has been cut out of the rectangle and rotated clockwise by 90 degrees. The small grey and white squares correspond to the number of grey and white shapes contained within the rectangle, respectively.

A – The grey shapes have been isolated and joined together, then coloured white.

159

C – The bottom row of three triangles is the same as the top three triangles if the entire top row was as a whole rotated 180 degrees and placed beneath itself, and then white triangles became black triangles and vice-versa.

160

C
A